PROBLEMS
OF POVERTY

AN INQUIRY
INTO THE INDUSTRIAL
CONDITION OF THE POOR

WITH AN EXCERPT FROM
Imperialism,
The Highest Stage Of Capitalism
BY V. I. LENIN

By

JOHN A. HOBSON

First published in 1891

This edition published by Read Books Ltd.
Copyright © 2019 Read Books Ltd.
This book is copyright and may not be
reproduced or copied in any way without
the express permission of the publisher in writing

British Library Cataloguing-in-Publication Data
A catalogue record for this book is available
from the British Library

CONTENTS

THE HIGHEST STAGE OF CAPITALISM

AN EXCERPT FROM
Imperialism,
The Highest Stage Of Capitalism
BY V. I. LENIN

During the past fifteen or twenty years, especially after the Spanish-American War (1898) and the Anglo-Boer War (1899-1902), the economic and also the political literature of the old and new world has more and more often adopted the term "imperialism" in order to characterise the epoch in which we live. In 1902, *Imperialism*, a work by English economist, J. A. Hobson, was published in London and New York. The author, who adopts the point of view of bourgeois social reformism and pacifism, which in essence is identical with the present position of the ex-Marxist, K. Kautsky, gives a very good and detailed description of the principal economic and political characteristics of imperialism.... Hobson, in his work on imperialism, marks the years 1884-1900 as being the period of intensified "expansion" of the chief European states. According to his estimate, England during these years acquired 3.7 million square miles of territory with a population of 57 million ; France acquired 3.6 million ; Germany one million square miles with 16.7 million inhabitants ; Belgium 900,000 square miles with 30 million inhabitants ; Portugal 800,000 square miles with 9 million inhabitants. The quest for colonies by all capitalist states at the end of the nineteenth century, and particularly since the 1880's, is a well-known fact in the history of diplomacy and of foreign policy.

PREFACE

The object of this volume is to collect, arrange, and examine some of the leading facts and forces in modern industrial life which have a direct bearing upon Poverty, and to set in the light they afford some of the suggested palliatives and remedies. Although much remains to be done in order to establish on a scientific basis the study of "the condition of the people," it is possible that the brief setting forth of carefully ascertained facts and figures in this little book may be of some service in furnishing a stimulus to the fuller systematic study of the important social questions with which it deals.

The treatment is designed to be adapted to the focus of the citizen-student who brings to his task not merely the intellectual interest of the collector of knowledge, but the moral interest which belongs to one who is a part of all he sees, and a sharer in the social responsibility for the present and the future of industrial society.

For the statements of fact contained in these chapters I am largely indebted to the valuable studies presented in the first volume of Mr. Charles Booth's *Labour and Life of the People*, a work which, when completed, will place the study of problems of poverty upon a solid scientific basis which has hitherto been wanting. A large portion of this book is engaged in relating the facts drawn from this and other sources to the leading industrial forces of the age.

In dealing with suggested remedies for poverty, I have selected certain representative schemes which claim to possess a present practical importance, and endeavoured to set forth briefly some of the economic considerations which bear upon their competency to achieve their aim. In doing this my object has been not to pronounce judgment, but rather to direct enquiry. Certain larger proposals of Land Nationalization and State Socialism, etc., I have left untouched, partly because it was impossible to deal, however briefly, even with the main issues involved in these questions, and partly because it seemed better to confine our enquiry to measures claiming a direct and present applicability.

In setting forth such facts as may give some measurement of the evils of Poverty, no attempt is made to suppress the statement of extreme cases which rest on sufficient evidence, for the nature of industrial poverty and the forces at work are often most clearly discerned and most rightly measured by instances which mark the severest pressure. So likewise there is no endeavour to exclude such human emotions as are "just, measured, and continuous," from the treatment of a subject where true feeling is constantly required for a proper realization of the facts.

In conclusion, I wish to offer my sincere thanks to Mr. Llewellyn Smith, Mr. William Clarke, and other friends who have been kind enough to render me valuable assistance in collecting the material and revising the proof-sheets of portions of this book.

PROBLEMS OF POVERTY

CHAPTER I.

THE MEASURE OF POVERTY.

§ 1. The National Income, and the Share of the Wage-earners.—To give a clear meaning and a measure of poverty is the first requisite. Who are the poor? The "poor law," on the one hand, assigns a meaning too narrow for our purpose, confining the application of the name to "the destitute," who alone are recognized as fit subjects of legal relief. The common speech of the comfortable classes, on the other hand, not infrequently includes the whole of the wage-earning class under the title of "the poor." As it is our purpose to deal with the pressure of poverty as a painful social disease, it is evident that the latter meaning is unduly wide. The "poor," whose condition is forcing "the social problem" upon the reluctant minds of the "educated" classes, include only the lower strata of the vast wage-earning class.

But since dependence upon wages for the support of life will be found closely related to the question of poverty, it is convenient to throw some preliminary light on the measure of poverty, by figures bearing on the general industrial condition of the wage-earning class. To measure poverty we must first measure wealth. What is the national income, and how is it divided? will naturally arise as the first questions. Now although the data for accurate measurement of the national income are somewhat slender, there is no very wide discrepancy in the results reached by the most skilful statisticians. For practical purposes we may regard the sum of £1,800,000,000 as fairly representing the national income. But when we put the further question, "How is this income divided among the various classes of the community?" we have to face wider discrepancies of judgment. The difficulties which beset a fair calculation of interest and profits, have introduced unconsciously a partisan element into the discussion. Certain authorities, evidently swayed by a desire to make the best of the present condition of the working-classes, have reached a low estimate of interest and profits, and a high estimate of wages; while others, actuated by a desire to emphasize the power of the capitalist classes, have minimized the share which goes as wages. At the outset of our inquiry, it might seem well to avoid such debatable ground. But the importance of the subject will not permit it to be thus shirked. The following calculation presents what is, in fact, a compromise of various views, and can only claim to be a rough approximation to the truth.

Taking the four ordinary divisions: Rent, as payment for the use of land, for agriculture, housing, mines, etc.; Interest for the use of business capital; Profit as wages of management and superintendence; and Wages, the weekly earnings of the working-classes, we find that the national income can be thus fairly apportioned—

Rent	£200,000,000.
Interest	£450,000,000.
Profits	£450,000,000.
Wages	£650,000,000.[1]
Total	£1750,000,000.

Professor Leone Levi reckoned the number of working-class families as 5,600,000, and their total income £470,000,000 in the year 1884.[2] If we now divide the larger money, minus

£650,000,000, among a number of families proportionate to the increase of the population, viz. 6,900,000, we shall find that the average yearly income of a working-class family comes to about £94, or a weekly earnings of about 36s. This figure is of necessity a speculative one, and is probably in excess of the actual average income of a working family.

This, then, we may regard as the first halting-place in our inquiry. But in looking at the average money income of a wage-earning family, there are several further considerations which vitally affect the measurement of the pressure of poverty.

First, there is the fact, that out of an estimated population of some 42,000,000, only 12,000,000, or about three out of every ten persons in the richest country of Europe, belong to a class which is able to live in decent comfort, free from the pressing cares of a close economy. The other seven are of necessity confined to a standard of life little, if at all, above the line of bare necessaries.

Secondly, the careful figures collected by these statisticians show that the national income equally divided throughout the community would yield an average income, per family, of about £182 per annum. A comparison of this sum with the average working-class income of £94, brings home the extent of inequality in the distribution of the national income. While it indicates that any approximation towards equality of incomes would not bring affluence, at anyrate on the present scale of national productivity, it serves also to refute the frequent assertions that poverty is unavoidable because Great Britain is not rich enough to furnish a comfortable livelihood for everyone.

§ 2. **Gradations of Working-class Incomes.**—But though it is true that an income of 36s. a week for an ordinary family leaves but a small margin for "superfluities," it will be evident that if every family possessed this sum, we should have little of the worst evils of poverty. If we would understand the extent of the disease, we must seek it in the inequality of incomes among the labouring classes themselves. No family need be reduced to suffering on 36s. a week. But unfortunately the differences of income among the working-classes are proportionately nearly as great as among the well-to-do classes. It is not merely the difference between the wages of skilled and unskilled labour; the 50s. per week of the high-class engineer, or typographer, and the 1s. 2d. per diem of the sandwich-man, or the difference between the wages of men and women workers. There is a more important cause of difference than these. When the average income of a working family is named, it must not be supposed that this represents the wage of the father of the family alone. Each family contains about 21/4 workers on an average. This is a fact, the significance of which is obvious. In some families, the father and mother, and one or two of the children, will be contributors to the weekly income; in other cases, the burden of maintaining a large family may be thrown entirely on the shoulders of a single worker, perhaps the widowed mother. If we reckon that the average wage of a working man is about 24s., that of a working woman 15s., we realize the strain which the loss of the male bread-winner throws on the survivor.

In looking at the gradations of income among the working-classes, it must be borne in mind that as you go lower down in the standard of living, each drop in money income represents a far more than proportionate increase of the pressure of poverty. Halve the income of a rich man, you oblige him to retrench; he must give up his yacht, his carriage, or other luxuries; but such retrenchment, though it may wound his pride, will not cause him great personal discomfort. But halve the income of a well-paid mechanic, and you reduce him and his family at once to the verge of starvation. A drop from 25s. to 12s. 6d. a week involves a vastly greater sacrifice than a drop from £500 to £250 a year. A working-class family, however comfortably it may live with a full contingent of regular workers, is almost always liable, by sickness, death, or loss of employment, to be reduced in a few weeks to a position of penury.

§ 3. Measurement of East London Poverty.—This brief account of the inequality of incomes has brought us by successive steps down to the real object of our inquiry, the amount and the intensity of poverty. For it is not inequality of income, but actual suffering, which moves the heart of humanity. What do we know of the numbers and the life of those who lie below the average, and form the lower orders of the working-classes?

Some years ago the civilized world was startled by the *Bitter Cry of Outcast London*, and much trouble has been taken of late to gauge the poverty of London. A host of active missionaries are now at work, engaged in religious, moral, and sanitary teaching, in charitable relief, or in industrial organization. But perhaps the most valuable work has been that which has had no such directly practical object in view, but has engaged itself in the collection of trustworthy information. Mr Charles Booth's book, *The Labour and Life of the People*, has an importance far in advance of that considerable attention which it has received. Its essential value is not merely that it supplies, for the first time, a large and carefully collected fund of facts for the formation of sound opinions and the explosion of fallacies, but that it lays down lines of a new branch of social study, in the pursuit of which the most delicate intellectual interests will be identified with a close and absorbing devotion to the practical issues of life.

In the study of poverty, the work of Mr. Booth and his collaborators may truly rank as an epoch-making work.

For the purpose we have immediately before us, the measurement of poverty, the figures supplied in this book are invaluable. Considerations of space will compel us to confine our attention to such figures as will serve to mark the extent and meaning of city poverty in London. But though, as will be seen, the industrial causes of London poverty are in some respects peculiar, there is every reason to believe that the extent and nature of poverty does not widely differ in all large centres of population.

The area which Mr. Booth places under microscopic observation covers Shoreditch, Bethnal Green, Whitechapel, St. George's in the East, Stepney, Mile End, Old Town, Poplar,

Hackney, and comprises a population 891,539. Of these no less than 316,000, or 35 per cent, belong to families whose weekly earnings amount to less than 21s. This 35 per cent, compose the "poor," according to the estimate of Mr. Booth, and it will be worth while to note the social elements which constitute this class. The "poor" are divided into four classes or strata, marked A, B, C, D. At the bottom comes A, a body of some 11,000, or 11/4 per cent, of hopeless, helpless city savages, who can only be said by courtesy to belong to the "working-classes" "Their life is the life of savages, with vicissitudes of extreme hardship and occasional excess. Their food is of the coarsest description, and their only luxury is drink. It is not easy to say how they live; the living is picked up, and what is got is frequently shared; when they cannot find 3d. for their night's lodging, unless favourably known to the deputy, they are turned out at night into the street, to return to the common kitchen in the morning. From these come the battered figures who slouch through the streets, and play the beggar or the bully, or help to foul the record of the unemployed; these are the worst class of corner-men, who hang round the doors of public-houses, the young men who spring forward on any chance to earn a copper, the ready materials for disorder when occasion serves. They render no useful service; they create no wealth; more often they destroy it."[3]

Next comes B, a thicker stratum of some 100,000, or 11½ per cent., largely composed of shiftless, broken-down men, widows, deserted women, and their families, dependent upon casual earnings, less than 18s. per week, and most of them incapable of regular, effective work. Most of the social wreckage of city life is deposited in this stratum, which presents the problem of poverty in its most perplexed and darkest form. For this class hangs as a burden on the shoulders of the more capable classes which stand just above it. Mr. Booth writes of it—

"It may not be too much to say that if the whole of class B were swept out of existence, all the work they do could be done, together with their own work, by the men, women, and children of classes C and D; that all they earn and spend might be earned, and could very easily be spent, by the classes above them; that these classes, and especially class C, would be immensely better off, while no class, nor any industry, would suffer in the least." Class C consists of 75,000, or 8 per cent., subsisting on intermittent earnings of from 18s. to 21s. for a moderate-sized family. Low-skilled labourers, poorer artizans, street-sellers, small shopkeepers, largely constitute this class, the curse of whose life is not so much low wages as irregularity of employment, and the moral and physical degradation caused thereby. Above these, forming the top stratum of "poor," comes a large class, numbering 129,000, or 14½ per cent., dependent upon small regular earnings of from 18s. to 21s., including many dock-and water-side labourers, factory and warehouse hands, car-men, messengers, porters, &c. "What they have comes in regularly, and except in times of sickness in the family, actual want rarely presses, unless the wife drinks."

"As a general rule these men have a hard struggle, but they are, as a body, decent, steady men, paying their way and bringing up their children respectably" (p. 50).

Mr Booth, in confining the title "poor" to this 35 per cent. of the population of East London, takes, perhaps for sufficient reasons, a somewhat narrow interpretation of the term. For in the same district no less than 377,000, or over 42 per cent. of the inhabitants, live upon earnings varying from 21s. to 30s. per week. So long as the father is in regular work, and his family is not too large, a fair amount of material comfort may doubtless be secured by those who approach the maximum. But such an income leaves little margin for saving, and innumerable forms of mishaps will bring such families down beneath the line of poverty. Though the East End contains more poverty than some other parts of London the difference is less than commonly supposed. Mr Booth estimated that of the total population of the metropolis 30.7 per cent. were living in poverty. The figure for York is placed by Mr Seebohm Rowntree[4] at the slightly lower figure of 27.84. These figures (in both cases exclusive of the population of the workhouses and other public or private institutions) may be taken as fairly representative of life in English industrial cities. A recent investigation of an ordinary agricultural village in Bedfordshire[5] discloses a larger amount of poverty—no less than 34.3 per cent. of the population falling below the income necessary for physical efficiency.

§ 4. **Prices for the Poor.**—These figures relating to money income do not bring home to us the evil of poverty. It is not enough to know what the weekly earnings of a poor family are, we must inquire what they can buy with them. Among the city poor, the evil of low wages is intensified by high prices. In general, the poorer the family the higher the prices it must pay for the necessaries of life. Rent is naturally the first item in the poor man's budget. Here it is evident that the poor pay in proportion to their poverty. The average rent in many large districts of East London is 4s. for one room, 7s. for two. In the crowded parts of Central London the figures stand still higher; 6s. is said to be a moderate price for a single room.[6] Mr. Marchant Williams, an Inspector of Schools for the London School Board, finds that 86 per cent. of the dwellers in certain poor districts of London pay more than one-fifth of their income in rent; 46 per cent. paying from one-half to one-quarter; 42 per cent. paying from one-quarter to one-fifth; and only 12 per cent. paying less than one-fifth of their weekly wage.[7] The poor from their circumstances cannot pay wholesale prices for their shelter, but must buy at high retail prices by the week; they are forced to live near their work (workmen's trains are for the aristocracy of labour), and thus compete keenly for rooms in the centres of industry; more important still, the value of central ground for factories, shops, and ware-houses raises to famine price the habitable premises. It is notorious that overcrowded, insanitary "slum" property is the most paying form of house property to its owners. The part played by rent in the problems of poverty can scarcely be over-estimated. Attempts to mitigate the evil by erecting model dwellings have scarcely touched the lower classes of wage-earners. The labourer prefers a room in a small house to an intrinsically better accommodation in a barrack-like building. Other than pecuniary motives enter in. The "touchiness of the lower class" causes them to be offended by the very sanitary regulations designed for their benefit.

But "shelter" is not the only thing for which the poor pay high. Astounding facts are adduced as to the prices paid by the poor for common articles of consumption, especially for vegetables, dairy produce, groceries, and coal. The price of fresh vegetables, such as carrots, parsnips, &c., in East London is not infrequently ten times the price at which the same articles can be purchased wholesale from the growers.[8]

Hence arises the popular cry against the wicked middleman who stands between producer and consumer, and takes the bulk of the profit. There is much want of thought shown in this railing against the iniquities of the middleman. It is true that a large portion of the price paid by the poor goes to the retail distributor, but we should remember that the labour of distribution under present conditions and with existing machinery is very great. We have no reason to believe that the small retailers who sell to the poor die millionaires. The poor, partly of necessity, partly by habit, make their purchases in minute quantities. A single family has been known to make seventy-two distinct purchases of tea within seven weeks, and the average purchases of a number of poor families for the same period amounted to twenty-seven. Their groceries are bought largely by the ounce, their meat or fish by the half-penn'orth, their coal by the cwt., or even by the lb. Undoubtedly they pay for these morsels a price which, if duly multiplied, represents a much higher sum than their wealthier neighbours pay for a much better article. But the small shopkeeper has a high rent to pay; he has a large number of competitors, so that the total of his business is not great; the actual labour of dispensing many minute portions is large; he is often himself a poor man, and must make a large profit on a small turn-over in order to keep going; he is not infrequently kept waiting for his money, for the amount of credit small shopkeepers will give to regular customers is astonishing. For all these, and many other reasons, it is easy to see that the poor man must pay high prices. Even his luxuries, his beer and tobacco, he purchases at exorbitant rates.

It is sometimes held sufficient to reply that the poor are thoughtless and extravagant. And no doubt this is so. But it must also be remembered that the industrial conditions under which these people live, necessitate a hand-to-mouth existence, and themselves furnish an education in improvidence.

§ 5. **Housing and Food Supply of the Poor.**—Once more, out of a low income the poor pay high prices for a bad article. The low physical condition of the poorest city workers, the high rate of mortality, especially among children, is due largely to the *quality*of the food, drink, and shelter which they buy. On the quality of the rooms for which they pay high rent it is unnecessary to dwell. Ill-constructed, unrepaired, overcrowded, destitute of ventilation and of proper sanitary arrangements, the mass of low class city tenements finds few apologists. The Royal Commission on Housing of the Working Classes thus deals with the question of overcrowding—

"The evils of overcrowding, especially in London, are still a public scandal, and are becoming in certain localities a worse scandal than they ever were. Among adults, overcrowding causes a vast amount of suffering which could be calculated by no bills of mortality, however accurate. The general deterioration in the health of the people is a worse feature of overcrowding even than the encouragement by it of infectious disease. It has the effect of reducing their stamina, and thus producing consumption and diseases arising from general debility of the system whereby life is shortened." "In Liverpool, nearly one-fifth of the squalid houses where the poor live in the closest quarters are reported to be always infected, that is to say, the seat of infectious diseases."

To apply the name of "home" to these dens is a sheer abuse of words. What grateful memories of tender childhood, what healthy durable associations, what sound habits of life can grow among these unwholesome and insecure shelters?

The city poor are a wandering tribe. The lack of fixed local habitation is an evil common to all classes of city dwellers. But among the lower working-classes "flitting" is a chronic condition. The School Board visitor's book showed that in a representative district of Bethnal Green, out of 1204 families, no less than 530 had removed within a twelvemonth, although such an account would not include the lowest and most "shifty" class of all. Between November 1885 and July 1886 it was found that 20 per cent. of the London electorate had changed residence. To what extent the uncertain conditions of employment impose upon the poor this changing habitation cannot be yet determined; but the absence of the educative influence of a fixed abode is one of the most demoralizing influences in the life of the poor. The reversion to a nomad condition is a retrograde step in civilization the importance of which can hardly be exaggerated. When we bear in mind that these houses are also the workshop of large numbers of the poor, and know how the work done in the crowded, tainted air of these dens brings as an inevitable portion of its wage, physical feebleness, disease, and an early death, we recognize the paramount importance of that aspect of the problem of poverty which is termed "The Housing of the Poor."

So much for the quality of the shelter for which the poor pay high prices. Turn to their food. In the poorest parts of London it is scarcely possible for the poor to buy pure food. Unfortunately the prime necessaries of life are the very things which lend themselves most easily to successful adulteration. Bread, sugar, tea, oil are notorious subjects of deception. Butter, in spite of the Margarine Act, it is believed, the poor can seldom get. But the systematic poisoning of alcoholic liquors permitted under a licensing System is the most flagrant example of the evil. There is some evidence to show that the poorer class of workmen do not consume a very large quantity of strong drink. But the vile character of the liquor sold to them acts on an ill-fed, unwholesome body as a poisonous irritant. We are told that "the East End dram-drinker has developed a new taste; it is for fusil-oil. It has even been said that ripe old whisky ten years old, drank in equal quantities, would probably import a tone of sobriety to the densely-populated quarters of East London."[9]

§ 6. **Irregularity of work.**—One more aspect of city poverty demands a word. Low wages are responsible in large measure for the evils with which we have dealt. In the life of the lower grades of labour there is a worse thing than low wages—that is irregular employment. The causes of such irregularity, partly inherent in the nature of the work, partly the results of trade fluctuations, will appear later. In gauging poverty we are only concerned with the fact. This irregularity of work is not in its first aspect so much a deficiency of work, but rather a maladjustment While on the one hand we see large classes of workers who are habitually overworked, men and women, tailors or shirt-makers in Whitechapel, 'bus men, shop-assistants, even railway-servants, toiling twelve, fourteen, fifteen, or even in some cases eighteen hours a day, we see at the same time and in the same place numbers of men and women seeking work and finding none. Thus are linked together the twin maladies of over-work and the unemployed. It is possible that among the comfortable classes there are still to be found those who believe that the unemployed consist only of the wilfully idle and worthless residuum parading a false grievance to secure sympathy and pecuniary aid, and who hold that if a man really wants to work he can always do so. This idle theory is contradicted by abundant facts. The official figures published by the Board of Trade gives the average percentage of unemployed in the Trade Unions of the skilled trades as follows. To the general average we have appended for comparison the average for the shipbuilding and boiler-making trades, so as to illustrate the violence of the oscillations in a fluctuating trade:—

	General per cent.	Ship-building, etc.
1884	7.15	20.8
1885	8.55	22.2
1886	9.55	21.6
1887	7.15	16.7
1888	4.15	7.3
1889	2.05	2.0
1890	2.10	3.4
1891	3.40	5.7
1892	6.20	10.9
1893	7.70	17.0
1894	7.70	16.2
1895	6.05	13.0
1896	3.50	9.5
1897	3.65	8.6
1898	3.15	4.7
1899	2.40	2.1
1900	2.85	2.3
1901	3.80	3.6
1902	4.60	8.3
1903	5.30	11.7

These figures make it quite evident that the permanent causes of irregular employment, e.g., weather in the building and riverside trades, season in the dressmaking and confectionery trades, and the other factors of leakage and displacement which throw out of work from time to time numbers of workers, are, taken in the aggregate, responsible only for a small proportion of the unemployment in the staple trades of the country.

The significance of such figures as these can scarcely be over-estimated. Although it might fairly be urged that the lowest dip in trade depression truly represented the injury inflicted on the labouring-classes by trade fluctuations, we will omit the year 1886, and take 1887 as a representative period of ordinary trade depression. The figures quoted above are supported by Trade Union statistics, which show that in that year among the strongest Trade Unions in the country, consisting of the picked men in each trade, no less than 71 in every 1000, or over 7 per cent., were continuously out of work. That this was due to their inability to get work, and not to their unwillingness to do it, is placed beyond doubt by the fact that they were, during this period of enforced idleness, supported by allowances paid by their comrades. Indeed, the fact that in 1890 the mass of unemployed was almost absorbed, disposes once for all of the allegation that the unemployed in times of depression consist of idlers who do not choose to work. Turning to the year 1887, there is every reason to believe that where 7 per cent, are unemployed in the picked, skilled industries of a country, where the normal supply of labour is actually limited by Union regulations, the proportion in unskilled or less organized industries is much larger. It is probable that 12 per cent, is not an excessive figure to take as the representative of the average proportion of unemployed. In the recent official returns of wages in textile industries, it is admitted that 10 per cent, should be taken off from the nominal wages for irregularity of employment. Moreover, it is true (with certain exceptions) that the lower you go down in the ranks of labour and of wages, the more irregular is the employment. To the pressure of this evil among the very poor in East London notice has already been drawn. We have seen how Mr. Booth finds one whole stratum of 100,000 people, who from an industrial point of view are worse than worthless. We have no reason to conclude that East London is much worse in this respect than other centres of population, and the irregularity of country employment is increasing every year. Are we to conclude then that of the thirteen millions composing the "working-classes" in this country, nearly two millions are liable at any time to figure as waste or surplus labour? It looks like it. We are told that the movements of modern industry necessitate the existence of a considerable margin supply of labour. The figures quoted above bear out this statement. But a knowledge of the cause does not make the fact more tolerable. We are not at present concerned with the requirements of the industrial machine, but with the quantity of hopeless, helpless misery these requirements indicate. The fact that under existing conditions the unemployed seem inevitable should afford the strongest motive for a change in these conditions. Modern life has no more tragical figure than the gaunt, hungry labourer wandering about the crowded centres of industry and wealth, begging in vain for permission to share in that industry, and to contribute to that wealth; asking in return not the comforts and luxuries of civilized life, but the rough food and shelter for himself and family, which would be practically secured to him in the rudest form of savage society.

Occasionally one of these sensational stories breaks into the light of day, through the public press, and shocks society at large, until it relapses into the consoling thought that such cases are exceptional. But those acquainted closely with the condition of our great cities know that there are thousands of such silent tragedies being played around us. In England the recorded deaths from starvation are vastly more numerous than in any other country. In 1880 the number for England is given as 101. In 1902 the number for London alone is 34. This is, of course, no adequate measure of the facts. For every recorded case there will be a hundred unrecorded cases where starvation is the practical immediate cause of death. The death-rate of children in the poorer districts of London is found to be nearly three times that which obtains among the richer neighbourhoods. Contemporary history has no darker page than that which records not the death-rate of children, but the conditions of child-life in our great cities. In setting down such facts and figures as may assist readers to adequately realize the nature and extent of poverty, it has seemed best to deal exclusively with the material aspects of poverty, which admit of some exactitude of measurement. The ugly and degrading surroundings of a life of poverty, the brutalizing influences of the unceasing struggle for bare subsistence, the utter absence of reasonable hope of improvement; in short, the whole subjective side of poverty is not less terrible because it defies statistics.

§ 7. **Figures and Facts of Pauperism.**—Since destitution is the lowest form of poverty, it is right to append to this statement of the facts of poverty some account of pauperism. Although chiefly owing to a stricter and wiser administration of the Poor Law in relation to outdoor relief, the number of paupers has steadily and considerably decreased, both in proportion to the population and absolutely, the number of those unable to support themselves is still deplorably large. In 1881 no less than one in ten of the total recorded deaths took place in workhouses, public hospitals, and lunatic asylums. In London the proportion is much greater and has increased during recent years. In 1901 out of 78,229 deaths in London, 13,009 took place in workhouses, 10,643 in public hospitals, and 349 in public asylums, making a total of 24,001. Comparing these figures with the total number of deaths, we find that in the richest city of the world 32.5 per cent., or one in three of the inhabitants, dies dependent on public charity. This estimate does not include those in receipt of outdoor relief. Moreover, it is an estimate which includes all classes. The proportion, taking the working-classes alone, must be even higher.

Turning from pauper deaths to pauper lives, the condition of the poor, though improved, is far from satisfactory. The agricultural labourer in many parts of England still looks to the poorhouse as a natural and necessary asylum for old age. Even the diminution effected in outdoor relief is not evidence of a corresponding decrease in the pressure of want. The diminution is chiefly due to increased strictness in the application of the Poor Law, a policy which in a few cases such as Whitechapel, Stepney, St. George-in-the-East, has succeeded in the practical extermination of the outdoor pauper. This is doubtless a wise policy, but it supplies no evidence of decrease in poverty. It would be possible by increased strictness of conditions to annihilate outdoor pauperism throughout the country at a single blow, and to reduce the number of indoor paupers by making workhouse life unendurable. But such a course would obviously furnish no satisfactory evidence of the decline of poverty, or even of destitution. Moreover, in regarding the decline of pauperism, we must not forget to take into account the enormous recent growth of charitable institutions and funds which now perform more effectually and more humanely much of the relief work which formerly devolved upon the Poor Law. The income of charitable London institutions engaged in promoting the physical well-being of the people amounted in 1902-3 to about four and a half millions. The relief afforded by Friendly Societies and Trade Unions to sick and out-of-work members, furnishes a more satisfactory evidence of the growth of providence and independence among all but the lowest classes of workers.

The improvement exhibited in figures of pauperism is entirely confined to outdoor relief. The number of workers who, by reason of old age or other infirmity, are compelled to take refuge in the poorhouses, bears a larger proportion to the total population than it did a generation ago. In 1876-7 the mean number of indoor paupers for England and Wales was 130,337, or 5.4 per 1000 of the population; in 1902-3 the number had risen to 203,604, or 6.2 per 1000 of the population. This rise of indoor pauperism has indeed been coincident with a larger decline of outdoor pauperism through this same period. But the growth of thrift in the working-classes, the increase of the machinery of charity, the rise of the average of wages—these causes have been wholly inoperative to check the growth of indoor pauperism. Nor, if one may trust so competent an authority as Mr Fowle, is this explained by any tendency of increased strictness in the administration of outdoor relief, to drive would-be recipients of outdoor relief into the workhouse.

The figures of London pauperism yield still more strange results. Here, though the percentage of paupers to population has shown a steady decline, the process has been so much slower than in the country that there has been no actual fall in the number of paupers. Throughout the whole period from 1861 to 1896 the numbers have remained about stationary, after which they show a considerable rise. The alarming feature in this table is the rapid rise of indoor pauperism, far more rapid than the growth of London's population. From 1861-2 the number of indoor paupers has grown by steady increase from 26,667 to 61,432 in 1902-3, or from a ratio of 9.5 to one of 13.4 per 1000. While the proportion of outdoor paupers per 1000 is little more than half that of the country as a whole, the proportion of indoor paupers is more than twice as great. Roughly speaking, London, with less than one-sixth of the population of the country, contains nearly one-third of the indoor pauperism. This fact alone throws some light upon the nature of city life. A close analysis of metropolitan workhouses discloses the fact that the aged, infirm, and children composed the vast majority of inmates. A very small percentage was found to be capable of actual work. About one-third of the paupers are children, about one-tenth lunatics, about one-half are aged, infirm, or sick. This leaves one-fifteenth as the proportion of able-bodied male and female adults. As a commentary on the administration of the Poor Law, these figures are eminently satisfactory, for they prove that people who can support themselves do not in fact obtain from public relief. But the picture has its dark side. It shows that a very large proportion of our workers, when their labour-power has been drained out of them, instead of obtaining a well-earned honourable rest, are obliged to seek refuge in that asylum which they and their class hate and despise. Whereas only 5 per cent of the population under 60 years are paupers, the proportion is 40 per cent in the case of those over 70. Taking the working-class only out of a population of 952,000 above the age of 65, no fewer than 402,000, or over 42 per cent, obtained relief in 1892. In London 22½ per cent of the aged poor are indoor paupers. The hardness of the battle of life is attested by this number of old men, and old women, who in spite of a hard-working life are compelled to end their days as the recipients of public charity.

§ 8. **The Diminution of Poverty in the last half century.**—
In order to realize the true importance of our subject, it is
necessary not only to have some measurement of the extent and
nature of poverty, but to furnish ourselves with some answer to
the question, Is this poverty increasing or diminishing? Until a
few years ago it was customary not only for platform agitators,
but for thoughtful writers on the subject, to assume that "the
rich are getting richer, and the poor are getting poorer." This
formula was ripening into a popular creed when a number of
statistical inquiries choked it. Prof. Leone Levi, Mr. Giffen, and
a number of careful investigators, showed a vast improvement
in the industrial condition of the working-classes during the
last half century. It was pointed out that money wages had
risen considerably in all kinds of employment; that prices had
generally fallen, so that the rise in real wages was even greater;
that they worked shorter hours; consumed more and better food;
lived longer lives; committed fewer crimes; and lastly, saved
more money. The general accuracy of these statements is beyond
question. The industrial conditions of the working-classes as
a whole shows a great advance during the last half century.
Although the evidence upon this point is by no means conclusive,
it seems probable that the income of the wage-earning classes
as an aggregate is growing even more rapidly than that of the
capitalist classes. Income-tax returns indicate that the proportion
of the population living on an acknowledged income of more
than £150 a year is much larger than it was a generation ago. In
1851 the income-tax-paying population amounted to 1,500,000;
in 1879-80 the number had risen to 4,700,000. At the same time
the average of these incomes showed a considerable fall, for while
in 1851 the gross income assessed was £272,000,000, in 1879-80
it had only risen to £577,000,000.

Though the method of assessing companies as if they
were single persons renders it impossible to obtain accurate
information in recent years as to the number of persons enjoying

incomes of various sizes, a comparison made by Mr Mulhall of incomes in 1867 and 1895 indicates that, while the lower middle-class is growing rapidly, the number of the rich is growing still more rapidly. While incomes of £100 to £300 have grown by a little more than 50 per cent., those from £300 to £1000 have nearly doubled, those between £1000 and £5000 have more than doubled, and incomes over £5000 have more than trebled.

But though such comparisons justify the conclusion that the upper grades of skilled labour have made considerable advances, and that the lower grades of regular unskilled labourers have to a less degree shared in this advance, they do not warrant the optimist conclusion often drawn from them, that poverty is a disease which left alone will cure itself, and which, in point of fact, is curing itself rapidly. Before we consent to accept the evidence of improvement in the average condition of the labouring classes during the last half century as sufficient evidence to justify this opinion we ought to pay regard to the following considerations—

1. It should be remembered that a comparison between England of the present day with England in the decade 1830-1840 is eminently favourable to a theory of progress. The period from 1790 to 1840 was the most miserable epoch in the history of the English working-classes. Much of the gain must be rightly regarded rather as a recovery from sickness, than as a growth in normal health. If the decade 1730-1740, for example, were to be taken instead, the progress of the wage-earner, especially in southern England, would be by no means so obvious. The southern agricultural labourer and the whole body of low-skilled workers were probably in most respects as well off a century and a half ago as they are to-day.

2. The great fall of prices, due to cheapening of production and of transport during the last twenty years, benefits the poor far less than the rich. For, while the prices of most comforts and luxuries have fallen very greatly, the same is not true of most necessaries. The gain to the workers is chiefly confined to food prices, which have fallen some 40 per cent since 1880. Taking

30

the retail prices of foods consumed by London working-class families we find that since 1880 the price of flour has fallen about 60 per cent., bread falling a little more than half that amount; the prices of beef and mutton have fallen nearly to the same extent as flour, though bacon stands in 1903 just about where it stood in 1880. Sugar exhibits a deep drop until 1898, rising afterwards in consequence of the war tax and the Sugar Convention; tea shows a not considerable drop. Other groceries, such as coffee and cocoa, and certain vegetables are cheaper. A careful inquiry into clothing shows a trifling fall of price for articles of the same quality, while the introduction of cheaper qualities has enabled workers to effect some saving here. Against these must be set a slight rise in price of dairy produce, a considerable rise in fuel, and a large rise in rent. A recent estimate of the Board of Trade, having regard to food, rent, clothing, fuel, and lighting as chief ingredients of working-class expenditure, indicates that 100 shillings will in 1900 do the work for which 120 shillings were required in 1880. The great fall of prices has been in the period 1880-1895, since then prices all round (except in clothing) show a considerable rise.

In turning from the working-classes as a whole to the poor, it becomes evident that the most substantial benefit they have received from falling prices is cheap bread. Cheap groceries and lighting are also gains, though it must be remembered that the modes of purchase to which the very poor are driven to have recourse minimize these gains. On clothes the poor spend a very small proportion of their incomes, the very poor virtually nothing. In the case of the lowest classes of the towns, it is probable that the rise in rents offsets all the advantages of cheapened prices for other commodities.

The importance of the bearing of this fact is obvious. Even were it clearly proved that the wages of the working-classes were increasing faster in proportion than the incomes of the wealthier classes, it would not be thereby shown that the standard of comfort in the former was rising as fast as the standard of comfort in the latter. If we confine the term "poor" to the lower grades of wage-earners, it would probably be correct to say that the riches of the rich had increased at a more rapid rate than that at which the poverty of the poor had diminished. Thus the width of the gap between riches and poverty would be absolutely greater than before. But, after all, such absolute measurements as these are uncertain, and have little other than a rhetorical value. What is important to recognize is this, that though the proportion of the very poor to the whole population has somewhat diminished, never in the whole history of England, excepting during the disastrous period at the beginning of this century, has the absolute number of the very poor been so great as it is now. Moreover, the massing of the poor in large centres of population, producing larger areas of solid poverty, presents new dangers and new difficulties in the application of remedial measures.

However we may estimate progress, one fact we must recognize, that the bulk of our low-skilled workers do not yet possess a secure supply of the necessaries of life. Few will feel inclined to dispute what Professor Marshall says on this point—

"The necessaries for the efficiency of an ordinary agricultural or of an unskilled town labourer and his family, in England, in this generation, may be said to consist of a well-drained dwelling with several rooms, warm clothing, with some changes of underclothing, pure water, a plentiful supply of cereal food, with a moderate allowance of meat and milk, and a little tea, &c.; some education, and some recreation; and lastly, sufficient freedom for his wife from other work to enable her to perform properly her maternal and her household duties. If in any district unskilled labour is deprived of any of these things, its efficiency will suffer in the same way as that of a horse which is not properly tended, or a steam-engine which has an inadequate supply of coals."[10]

There is one final point of deep significance. So far we have endeavoured to measure poverty by the application of a standard of actual material comfort. But this, while furnishing a fair gauge of the deprivation suffered by the poor, does not enable us to measure it as a social danger. There is a depth of poverty, of misery, of ignorance, which is not dangerous because it has no outlook, and is void of hope. Abate the extreme stress of poverty, give the poor a glimpse of a more prosperous life, teach them to know their power, and the danger of poverty increases. This is what De Tocqueville meant when writing of France, before the Revolution, he said, "According as prosperity began to dawn in France, men's minds appeared to become more unquiet and disturbed; public discontent was sharpened, hatred of all ancient institutions went on increasing, till the nation was visibly on the verge of a revolution. One might almost say that the French found their condition all the more intolerable according as it became better."[11]

So in England the change of industrial conditions which has massed the poor in great cities, the spread of knowledge by compulsory education, cheap newspapers, libraries, and a thousand other vehicles of knowledge, the possession and growing appreciation of political power, have made poverty more self-conscious and the poor more discontented. By striving to educate, intellectually, morally, sanitarily, the poor, we have made them half-conscious of many needs they never recognized before. They were once naked, and not ashamed, but we have taught them better. We have raised the standard of the requirements of a decent human life, but we have not increased to a corresponding degree their power to attain them. If by poverty is meant the difference between felt wants and the power to satisfy them, there is more poverty than ever. The income of the poor has grown, but their desires and needs have grown more rapidly. Hence the growth of a conscious class hatred, the "growing animosity of the poor against the rich," which Mr. Barnett notes in the slums of Whitechapel. The poor were once too stupid and too sodden for vigorous discontent, now though their poverty may be less intense, it is more alive, and more militant. The rate of improvement in the condition of the poor is not quick enough to stem the current of popular discontent.

Nor is it the poor alone who are stricken with discontent. Clearer thought and saner feelings are beginning to make it evident that in the march of true civilization no one class can remain hopelessly behind. Hence the problems of poverty are ever pressing more and more upon the better-hearted, keener-sighted men and women of the more fortunate classes; they feel that *they* have no right to be contented with the condition of the poor. The demand that a life worth living shall be made possible for all, and that the knowledge, wealth, and energy of a nation shall be rightly devoted to no other end than this, is the true measure of the moral growth of a civilized community. The following picture drawn a few years ago by Mr. Frederick Harrison shows how far we yet fall short of such a realization— "To me at least, it would be enough to condemn modern society as hardly an advance on slavery or serfdom, if the permanent condition of industry were to be that which we now behold; that 90 per cent, of the actual producers of wealth have no home that they can call their own beyond the end of a week; have no bit of soil, or so much as a room that belongs to them; have nothing of value of any kind except as much as will go in a cart; have the precarious chance of weekly wages which barely suffice to keep them in health; are housed for the most part in places that no man thinks fit for his horse; are separated by so narrow a margin from destitution that a month of bad trade, sickness, or unexpected loss brings them face to face with hunger and pauperism."[12]

CHAPTER II.

THE EFFECTS OF MACHINERY ON THE CONDITION OF THE WORKING-CLASSES.

§ 1. **Centralizing-Influence of Machinery.**—In seeking to understand the nature and causes of the poverty of the lower working-classes, it is impossible to avoid some discussion of the influence of machinery. For the rapid and continuous growth of machinery is at once the outward visible sign and the material agent of the great revolution which has changed the whole face of the industrial world during the last century. With the detailed history of this vast change we are not concerned, but only with its effects on the industrial condition of the poor in the present day.

Those who have studied in books of history the industrial and educational condition of the mass of the working populace at the beginning of this century, or have read such novels as *Shirley*, *Mary Barton*, and *Alton Locke*, will not be surprised at the mingled mistrust and hatred with which the working-classes regarded each new introduction of machinery into the manufacturing arts. These people, having only a short life to live, naturally took a short-sighted view of the case; having a specialized form of skill as their only means of getting bread, they did not greet with joy the triumphs of inventive skill which robbed this skill of its market value. Even the more educated champions of the interests of working-classes have often viewed with grave suspicion the rapid substitution of machinery for hand-labour in the industrial arts. The enormous increase of wealth-producing power given by the new machinery can scarcely be realized. It is reckoned that fifty men with modern machinery could do all the cotton-spinning of the whole of Lancashire a century ago. Mr. Leone Levi has calculated that to make by hand all the yarn spun in England in one year by the use of the self-acting mule, would take 100,000,000 men. The instruments which work this wonderful change are called "labour-saving" machinery. From this title it may be deemed that their first object, or at any rate their chief effect, would be to lighten labour. It seems at first sight therefore strange to find so reasonable a writer as John Stuart Mill declaring, "It is questionable if all the mechanical inventions yet made have lightened the day's toil of any human being." Yet if we confine our attention to the direct effects of machinery, we shall acknowledge that Mill's doubt is, upon the whole, a well founded one.

According to the evidence of existing poverty adduced in the last chapter, it would appear that the lowest classes of workers have not shared to any considerable degree the enormous gain of wealth-producing power bestowed by machinery. It is not our object here to discuss the right of the poorer workers to profit by inventions due to others, but merely to indicate the effects which the growth of machinery actually produce in this economic condition. Let us examine the industrial effects of the growth of machinery, so as to understand how they affect the social and economic welfare of the working-classes.

§ 2. Class Separation of Employer and Workmen.—The first effect of machinery is to give a new and powerful impulse to the centralizing tendency in industry. "Civilization is economy of power, and English power is coal," said the materialistic Baron Liebig. Coal as a generator of steam-power demands that manufactures shall be conducted on a large scale in particular localities. Before the day of large, expensive steam-driven machinery, manufacture was done in scattered houses by workers who were the owners of their simple tools, and often of the material on which they worked; or in small workshops, where a master worked with a few journeymen and apprentices. Machinery changed all this. It drove the workers into large factories, and obliged them to live in concentrated masses near their work. They no longer owned the material in which their labour was stored, or the tools with which they worked; they had to use the material belonging to their employer; the machinery which made their tools valueless was also the property of the capitalist employer. Instead of selling the products of their capital and labour to merchants or consumers, they were compelled to sell their labour-power to the employer as the only means of earning a livelihood. Again, the social relations between the wealthy employer and his "hands" were quite different from those intimate personal relations which had subsisted between the small master and his assistants. The very size of the factory made such a social change inevitable, the personal relation which marked medieval industry was no longer possible. Machinery then did two things. On the one hand, it destroyed the position of the workman as a self-sufficing industrial unit, and made him dependent on a capitalist for employment and the means of supporting life. On the other hand, it weakened the sense of responsibility in the employer towards his workmen in proportion as the dependence of the latter became more absolute.

With each step in the growth of the factory system the workman became more dependent, and the employer more irresponsible. Thus we note the first industrial effect of machinery in the formation of two definite industrial classes— the dependent workman, and the irresponsible employer. The term "irresponsible" is not designed to convey any moral stigma. The industrial employer can no more be blamed for being irresponsible than the workman for being dependent. The terms merely express the nature of the schism which naturally followed the triumph of machinery. Prophets like Carlyle and Ruskin, slighting the economic causes of the change, clamoured for "Captains of Industry," employers who should realize a moral responsibility, and reviving a dead feudalism should assume unasked the protectorate of their employés. The whole army of theoretic and practical reformers might indeed be divided into two classes, according as they seek to impose responsibility on employers, or to establish a larger independence in the employed. But this is not the place to discuss methods of reform. It is sufficient to note the testimony borne by all alike to the disintegrating influence of machinery.

Again, the growth of machinery makes industry more intricate. Manufacturers no longer produce for a small known market, the fluctuations of which are slight, and easily calculable. The element of speculation enters into manufacture at every pore—size of market, competitors, and price are all unknown. Machinery works at random like the blind giant it is. Every improvement in communication, and each application of labour-saving invention adds to the delicacy and difficulty of trade calculations. Hence in the productive force of machinery we see the material cause of the violent oscillations, the quiver of which never has time to pass out of modern trade. The periodic over-production and subsequent depression are thus closely related to machinery. It is the result upon the workman of these fluctuations that alone concerns us.

The effect of machinery upon the regularity of employment is both a difficult and a serious subject. Its precise importance cannot be measured. Before the era of machinery there often arose from other reasons, especially war or failure of crops, fluctuations which worked most disastrously on the English labourer. But in modern times we must look to more distinctively industrial causes for an explanation of unsteadiness of employment, and here the close competition of steam-driven machinery plays the leading part.

It must not, however, be supposed that machinery is essentially related to unsteadiness of work. The contrary is obviously the case. Cheap tools can be kept idle without great loss to their owner, but every stoppage in the work of expensive machinery means a heavy loss to the capitalist. Thus the larger the part played by expensive machinery, the stronger the personal motive in the individual capitalist to give full regular employment to his workmen. It is the competition of other machinery over which he has no control that operates as the immediate cause of instability of work. Thus the growth of machinery has a double and conflicting influence upon regularity of employment; it punishes capital more severely for each irregularity or stoppage, while at the same time it makes such fluctuations more violent.

§ 3. **Displacement of Labour.**—But the result of machinery which has drawn most attention is the displacement of labour. In every branch of productive work, agriculture as well as manufacture, the conflict between manual skill and machine skill has been waged incessantly during the last century. Step by step all along the line the machine has ousted the skilled manual worker, either rendering his office superfluous, or retaining him to play the part of servant to the new machine. A good deal of thoughtless rhetoric has been consumed upon the subject of this new serfdom of the worker to machinery. There is no reason in the nature of things why the work of attendance on machinery should not be more dignified, more pleasant, and more remunerative to the working-man than the work it displaces. To shift on to the shoulders of brute nature the most difficult and exhausting kinds of work has been in large measure the actual effect of machinery. There is also every reason to believe that the large body of workers whose work consists in the regular attendance on and manipulation of machinery have shared largely in the results of the increased production which machinery has brought about. The present "aristocracy of labour" is the direct creation of the machine. But our concern lies chiefly with the weaker portion of the working-classes. How does the constant advance of labour-saving machinery affect these? What is the effect of machinery upon the demand for labour? In answering these questions we have to carefully distinguish the ultimate effect upon the labour-market as a whole, and the immediate effect upon certain portions of the labour-supply.

It is generally urged that machinery employs as many men as it displaces. This has in fact been the earlier effect of the introduction of machinery into the great staple industries of the country. The first effect of mechanical production in the spinning and weaving industries was to displace the hand-worker. But the enormous increase in demand for textile wares caused by the fall of price, has provided work for more hands than were employed before, especially when we bear in mind the subsidiary work in construction of machinery, and enlarged mechanism of conveyance and distribution. Taking a purely historical view of the question, one would say that the labour displaced by machinery found employment in other occupations, directly or indirectly, due to the machinery itself. Provided the aggregate volume of commerce grows at a corresponding pace with the labour-saving power of new machinery, the classes dependent on the use of their labour have nothing in the long run to fear.

A machine is invented which will enable one man to make as many boots as four men made formerly, displacing the labour of three men. If the cheapening of boots thus brought about doubles the sale of boots, one of the three "displaced" men can find employment at the machine. If it takes the labour of one man to keep up the production of the new machinery, and another to assist in the distribution of the increased boot-supply, it will be evident that the aggregate of labour has not suffered. It is, however, clear that this exactly balanced effect by no means necessarily happens. The expansion of consumption of commodities produced by machinery is not necessarily such as to provide employment for the displaced labour in the same trade or its subsidiary trades. The result of the introduction of machinery may be a displacement of human by mechanical labour, so far as the entire trade is concerned. The bearing of this tendency is of great significance. Analysis of recent census returns shows that not only is agriculture rapidly declining in the amount of employment it affords, but that the same tendency occurs in the staple processes of manufacture: either there is an absolute decline in employment, as in the textile and dress trades, or the rate of increase is considerably slower than that of the occupied class as a whole, indicating a relative decline of importance. This tendency is greatest where machinery is most highly developed—that is to say, machinery has kept out of these industries a number of workers who in the ordinary condition of affairs would have been required to assist in turning out the increased supply. The recent increase of population has been shut out of the staple industries. They are not therefore compelled to be idle. Employment for these has been found chiefly in satisfying new wants. But industries engaged in supplying new wants, i.e. new comforts or new luxuries, are obviously less steady than those engaged in supplying the prime necessaries of ordinary life.

Thus while it may be true that the ultimate effect of the introduction of machinery is not to diminish the demand for labour, it would seem to operate in driving a larger and larger proportion of labour to find employment in those industries which from their nature furnish a less steady employment. Again, though the demand for labour may in the long run always keep pace with the growth of machinery, it is obvious that the workers whose skill loses its value by the introduction of machinery must always be injured. The process of displacement in particular trades has been responsible for a large amount of actual hardship and suffering among the working-classes.

It is little comfort to the hand-worker, driven out to seek unskilled labour by the competition of new machinery, that the world will be a gainer in the long run. "The short run, if the expression may be used, is often quite long enough to make the difference between a happy and a miserable life."[13] Philosophers may reckon this evil as a part of the inevitable price of progress, but it is none the less deplorable for that. Society as a whole gains largely by each step; a small number of those who can least afford to lose, are the only losers.

The following quotation from an address given at the Industrial Remuneration Congress in 1886, puts the case with admirable clearness—"The citizens of England are too intelligent to contend against such cheapening of production, as they know the result has been beneficial to mankind; but many of them think it is a hardship and injustice which deserves more attention that those whose skilled labour is often superseded by machinery, should have to bear all the loss and poverty through their means to earn a living being taken away from them. If there is a real vested interest in existence which entitles to compensation in some form when it is interfered with, it is that of a skilled producer in his trade; for that skill has not only given him a living, but has added to the wealth and prosperity of the community."[14] The quantity of labour displaced by machinery and seeking new employment, forms a large section of the margin of unemployed, and will form an important factor in the problem of poverty.

§ 4. **Effect of Machinery upon the Character of Labour.**
Next, what is the general effect of machinery upon the character of the work done? The economic gain attending all division of labour is of course based on the improved quality and quantity of work obtained by confining each worker to a narrow range of activity. If no great inventions in machinery took place, we might therefore expect a constant narrowing of the activity of each worker, which would make his work constantly more simple, and more monotonous, and himself more and more dependent on the regular co-operation of an increasing number of other persons over whom he had no direct control. Without the growth of modern machinery, mere subdivision of labour would constantly make for the slavery and the intellectual degradation of labour. Independently of the mighty and ever-new applications of mechanical forces, this process of subdivision or specialization would take place, though at a slower pace. How far does machinery degrade, demoralize, dementalize the worker?

The constantly growing specialization of machinery is the most striking industrial phenomenon of modern times. Since the worker is more and more the attendant of machinery, does not this mean a corresponding specialization of the worker? It would seem so at first sight, yet if we look closer it becomes less obvious. So far as mere manual activity is concerned, it seems probable that the general effect of machinery has been both to narrow the range of that activity, and to take over that dexterity which consisted in the incessant repetition of a single uniform process. Very delicately specialized manipulation is precisely the work it pays best to do by machinery, so that, as Professor Marshall says, "machinery can make uniform actions more accurately and effectively than man can; and most of the work which was done by those who were specially skilful with the fingers a few generations ago, is now done by machinery."[15] He illustrates from the wood and metal industries, where the process is constantly going on.

"The chief difficulty to be overcome is that of getting the machinery to hold the material firmly in exactly the position in which the machine-tool can be brought to bear on it in the right way, and without wasting meanwhile too much time in taking grip of it. But this can generally be contrived when it is worth while to spend some labour and expense on it; and then the whole operations can often be controlled by a worker, who, sitting before the machine, takes with the left hand a piece of wood or metal from a heap, and puts it in a socket, while with the right he draws down a lever, or in some other way sets the machine-tool at work, and finally with his left hand throws on to another heap the material which has been cut, or punched, or drilled, or planed exactly after a given pattern."

Professor Marshall summarizes the tendency in the following words—"We are thus led to a general rule, the action of which is more prominent in some branches of manufacture than others, but which applies to all. It is, that any manufacturing operation that can be reduced to uniformity, so that the same thing has to be done over and over again in the same way, is sure to be taken over sooner or later by machinery. There may be delays and difficulties; but if the work to be done by it is on a sufficient scale, money and inventive power will be spent without stint on the task till it is achieved. There still remains the responsibility for seeing that the machinery is in good order and working smoothly; but even this task is often made light of by the introduction of an automatic movement which brings the machine to a stop the instant anything goes wrong."[16]

Since the economy of production constantly induces machinery to take over all work capable of being reduced to routine, it would seem to follow by a logical necessity that the work left for the human worker was that which was less capable of being subjected to close uniformity; that is work requiring discretion and intelligence to be applied to each separate action. Although the process described by Professor Marshall assigns a constantly diminishing proportion of each productive work to the effort of man, of that portion which remains for him to do a constantly increasing proportion will be work of judgment and specific calculation applied to particular cases. And this is the conclusion which Professor Marshall himself asserts—

"Since machinery does not encroach much upon that manual work which requires judgment, while the management of machinery does require judgment, there is a much greater demand now than formerly for intelligence and resource. Those qualities which enable men to decide rightly and quickly in new and difficult cases, are the common property of the better class of workmen in almost every trade, and a person who has acquired them in one trade can easily transfer them to another."

If this is true, it signifies that the formal specialization of the worker, which comes from his attendance on a more and more specialized piece of machinery, does not really narrow and degrade his industrial life, but supplies a certain education of the judgment and intelligence which has a general value that more than compensates the apparent specialization of manual functions. The very fact that the worker's services are still required is a proof that his work is less automatic (i.e. more intelligent) than that of the most delicate machinery in use; and since the work which requires less intelligence is continually being taken over by machinery, the work which remains would seem to require a constantly higher average of intelligence. It is, of course, true that there are certain kinds of work which can never be done by machinery, because they require a little care and a little judgment, while that care and judgment is so slight as to supply no real food for thought, or education for the judgment. No doubt a good deal of the less responsible work connected with machinery is of this order. Moreover, there are certain other influences to be taken into account which affect the net resuit of the growth of machinery upon the condition of the workers. The physical and moral evils connected with the close confinement of large bodies of workers, especially in the case of young persons, within the narrow unwholesome limits of the factory or mill, though considerably mitigated by the operation of factory legislation, are still no light offset against the advantages which have been mentioned. The weakly, ill-formed bodies, the unhealthy lives lived by the factory-workers in our great manufacturing centres are facts which have an intimate connection with the growth of machinery. But though our agricultural population, in spite of their poverty and hard work, live longer and enjoy better physical health than our town-workers, there are few who would deny that the town-workers are both better educated and more intelligent. This intelligence must in a large measure be attributed to the influences of machinery, and of those social conditions which machinery has assisted to establish. This intelligence must be reckoned as an adequate offset against the formal specialization of machine-labour, and must be regarded as an emancipative influence, giving to its possessor a larger choice in the forms of employment. So far as a man's labour-power consists in the mere knowledge how to tend a particular piece of machinery he may appear to be more "enslaved" with each specialization of machinery; but so far as his labour-power consists in the practice of discretion and intelligence, these are qualities which render him more free.

Moreover, as regards the specialization of machinery, there is one point to be noticed which modifies to some considerable extent the effects of subdivision upon labour. On the one hand, the tendency to split up the manufacture of a commodity into several distinct branches, often undertaken in different localities and with wholly different machinery, prevents the skilled worker in one branch from passing into another, and thus limits his practical freedom as an industrial worker. On the other hand, this has its compensating advantage in the tendency of different trades to adopt analogous kinds of machinery and similar processes. Thus, while a machinist engaged in a screw manufactory is so specialized that he cannot easily pass from one process to another process in the screw trade, he will find himself able to obtain employment in other hardware manufactures which employ the same or similar processes.

§ 5. **Are all Men equal before the Machine?**—It is sometimes said that "all men become equal before the machine." This is only true in the sense that there are certain large classes of machine-work which require in the worker such attention, care, endurance, and skill as are within the power of most persons possessed of ordinary capacities of mind and body. In such forms of machine-work it is sometimes possible for women and children to compete with men, and even to take their places by their ability to offer their work at a cheaper price. The effect of machinery development in thus throwing on the labour-market a large quantity of women and children competitors is one of those serious questions which will occupy our attention in a later chapter. It is here sufficient to remember that it was this effect which led to a general recognition of the fact that machinery and the factory system could not be trusted to an unfettered system of *laissez faire*. The Factory Acts, and the whole body of legislative enactments, interfering with "freedom of contract" between employer and employed, resulted from the fact that machinery enabled women and children to be employed in many branches of productive work from which their physical weakness precluded them before.

§ 6. **Summary of Effects of Machinery on the Condition**

of the Poor.—To sum up with any degree of precision the net advantages and disadvantages of the growth of machinery upon the working classes is impossible. If we look not merely at the growth of money incomes, but at the character of those products which have been most cheapened by the introduction of machinery, we shall incline to the opinion that the net gain in wealth-producing power due to machinery has not been equally shared by all classes in the community.[17]

The capitalist classes, so far as they can be properly severed from the rest of the community, have gained most, as was inevitable in a change which increased the part played by capital in production. A short-timed monopoly of the abnormal profits of each new invention, and an enormous expansion of the field of investment for capital must be set against the gradual fall in the interest paid for the use of each piece of capital. But as the advantage of each new invention has by the competition of machinery-owners been passed on to the consumer, all other classes of the community have gained in proportion to their consumption of machinery-produced commodities. As machinery plays a smaller part in the production of necessaries of life than in the production of comforts and luxuries, it will be evident that each class gain as consumers in proportion to its income. The poorest classes, whose consumption of machine-productions is smallest, gain least. It cannot, however, be said, that there is any class of regular workers who, as consumers, have been injured by machinery. All have gained. The skilled workmen, the aristocracy of labour, have, as has been shown, gained very considerably. Even the poor classes of regular unskilled workmen have raised their standard of comfort.

It is in its bearing on the industrial condition of the very poor, and those who are unable to get regular work at decent wages, that the influence of machinery is most questionable. Violent trade fluctuations, and a continuous displacement of hand-labour by new mechanical inventions, keep in perpetual existence a large margin of unemployed or half-employed, who form the most hopeless and degraded section of the city poor, and furnish a body of reckless, starving competitors for work, who keep down the standard of wages and of life for the lower grades of regular workers affected by this competition.

CHAPTER III.

THE INFLUX OF POPULATION INTO LARGE TOWNS.

§ 1. Movements of Population between City and Country.
The growth of large cities is so closely related to the problems of poverty as to deserve a separate treatment. The movements of population form a group of facts more open than most others to precise measurement, and from them much light is thrown on the condition of the working classes. That the towns are growing at the expense of the country, is a commonplace to which we ought to seek to attach a more definite meaning.

We may trace the inflow of country-born people into the towns by looking either at the statistics of towns, or of rural districts. But first we ought to bear in mind one fact. Quite apart from any change in proportion of population, there is an enormous interchange constantly taking place between adjoining counties and districts. The general fluidity of population has been of course vastly increased by new facilities of communication and migration; persons are less and less bound down to the village or county in which they were born. So we find that in England and Wales, only 739 out of each 1000 persons were living in their native county in 1901. In some London districts it is reckoned that more than one quarter of the inhabitants change their address each year. So that when we are told that in seven large Scotch towns only 524 out of each 1000 are natives, and that in Middlesex only 35 per cent. of the male adult population are Middlesex by birth, we are not thereby enabled to form any conclusion as to the growth of towns.

To arrive at any useful result we must compare the inflow

with the outflow. Most of the valuable information we possess on this point applies directly to London but the same forces which are operating in London, will be found to be at work with more or less intensity in other centres of population in proportion to their size. Comparing the inflow of London with its outflow, we find that in 1881 nearly twice as many strangers were living in London as Londoners were living outside; in other words, that London was gaining from the country at the rate of more than 10,000 per annum. So far as London itself is concerned, the last two censuses show a cessation of the flow, but the enormous growth of Middlesex outside the metropolitan boundaries indicates a continuance of the centripetal tendency.

Now what does London do with this increase? Is it spread evenly over the surface of the great city?

Certainly not. And here we reach a point which has a great significance for those interested in East London. It is clearly shown that none of this gain goes to swell the numbers of East London. Many individual strangers of course go there, but the outflow from East London towards the suburban parts more than compensates the inflow. By comparing the population of East London in 1901 with that in 1881, it is found that the increase is far less than it ought to be, if we add the excess of births over deaths. How is this? The answer is not far to seek, and stamps with fatal significance one aspect of Poverty, namely, overcrowding. East London does not gain so fast as other parts, because it will not hold any more people. It has reached what is termed "saturation point." Introduce strangers, and they can only stay on condition that they push out, and take the place of, earlier residents.

So we find in all districts of large towns, where poverty lies thickest, the inflow is less than the outflow. The great stream of incomers goes to swell the population of parts not hitherto overcrowded, thus ever increasing the area of dense city population. Districts like Bethnal Green and Mile End are found to show the smallest increase, while outlying districts like West

Ham grow at a prodigious pace.

§ 2. **Rate of Migration from Rural Districts.**—But perhaps the most instructive point of view from which to regard the absorption of country population by the towns is not from inside but from outside.

Confining our attention for the present to migration from the country to the town, and leaving the foreign immigration for separate treatment, we find that the large majority of incomers to London are from agricultural counties, such as Kent, Bucks, Herts, Devon, Lincoln, and not from counties with large manufacturing centres of their own, like Yorkshire, Lancashire, and Cheshire. The great manufacturing counties contribute very slightly to the growth of London. While twelve representative agricultural counties furnished sixteen per 1000 of the population of London in 1881, twelve representative manufacturing counties supplied no more than two-and-a-half per 1000.

Respecting the rate of the decline of agricultural population exaggerated statements are often made. If we take the inhabitants of rural sanitary districts, and of urban districts below 10,000 as the rural population, we shall find that between 1891 and 1901 the growth in the rural districts is 5.3 per cent. as compared with 15.8 per cent. for the centres of population. Even if the urban standard be placed at a lower point, 5000, there is still an increase of 3.5 per cent. in the rural population. If, however, we eliminate the "home" counties and other rural districts round the large centres of population, largely used for residential purposes, and turn to agricultural England, we shall find that it shows a positive decline in rural population. In the period 1891-1901 no fewer than 18 English and Welsh counties show a decrease of rural inhabitants, taking the higher limit of urban population. This has been going on with increasing rapidity during the last forty years. Whereas, in 1861, 37.7 per cent. of the population were living in the country, in 1901 the proportion has sunk to 23 per cent.

What these figures mean is that almost the whole of the

natural increase in country population is being gradually sucked into city life. Not London alone, of course, but all the large cities have been engaged in this work of absorption. Everywhere the centripetal forces are at work. The larger the town the stronger the power of suction, and the wider the area over which the attraction extends. There are three chief considerations which affect the force with which the attraction of a large city acts upon rural districts. The first is distance. By far the largest quantity of new-comers into London are natives of Middlesex, Kent, Bucks, and what are known as "the home counties." As we pass further North and West, the per-centage gradually though not quite regularly declines. The numbers from Durham and Northumberland on the one hand, and from Devon and Somerset on the other are much larger than those from certain nearer counties, such as Stafford, Yorkshire, and Lancaster. The chief determinate of the force of attraction, distance from the centre, is in these cases qualified by two other considerations. In the case of Durham and Northumberland a large navigable seaboard affords greater facility and cheapness of transport, an important factor in the mobility of labour. In the case of Devon and Somerset the absence of the counter-attraction of large provincial cities drives almost the whole of its migratory folk to London, whereas in Yorkshire and Lancashire and the chief Midland manufacturing counties the attraction of their own industrial centres acts more powerfully in their immediate neighbourhood than the magic of London itself. Thus, if we were to take the map of England and mark it so as to represent the gravitation towards cities, we should find that every remotest village was subject to a number of weaker or stronger, nearer or more distant, forces, which were helping to draw off its rising population into the eddy of city life. If we examined in detail a typical agricultural county, we should probably find that while its one or two considerable towns of 40,000 or 50,000 inhabitants were growing at something above the average rate for the whole country, the smaller towns of 5000 to 10,000 were only just managing to hold their own, the smallest towns and large villages were steadily declining, while the scattered agricultural population remained almost stationary. For it is the small towns and the villages that suffer most, for reasons which will shortly appear.

§ 3. **Effects of Agricultural Depression.**—We have next to ask what is the nature of this attractive force which drains the country to feed the city population? What has hitherto been spoken of as a single force will be seen to be a complex of several forces, different in kind, acting conjointly to produce the same result.

The first readily suggests itself couched under the familiar phrase, Agricultural Depression. It is needless here to enlarge on this big and melancholy theme. It is evident that what is called the law of Diminishing Return to Labour in Agriculture, the fact that every additional labourer, upon a given surface, beyond a certain sufficient number, will be less and less profitably employed, while the indefinite expansion of manufacture will permit every additional hand to be utilized so as to increase the average product of each worker, would of itself suffice to explain why in a fairly thickly populated country like England, young labourers would find it to their interest to leave the land and seek manufacturing work in the cities. This would of itself explain why the country population might stand still while the city grew. When to this natural tendency we add the influence of the vast tracts of virgin, or cheaply cultivated soil, brought into active competition with English agriculture by the railways and steamships which link us with distant lands in America, Australia, and Asia, we have a fully adequate explanation of the main force of the tide in the movement of population. After a country has reached a certain stage in the development of its resources, the commercial population must grow more quickly than the agricultural, and the larger the outside area open to supply agricultural imports the faster the change thus brought about in the relation of city and rural population.

§ 4. **Nature of the Decline of Rural Population.**—It has been shown that the absolute reduction in the number of those living in rural districts is very small. If, however, we take the statistics of farmers and farm-labourers in these same districts we often find a very considerable decline. The real extent of the decline of agriculture is somewhat concealed by the habit of including in the agricultural population a good many people not engaged in work of agriculture. The number of retail shopkeepers, railway men and others concerned with the transport of goods, domestic servants, teachers, and others not directly occupied in the production of material wealth, has considerably increased of late years. So too, not every form of agriculture has declined. While farmers and labourers show a decrease, market-gardeners show a large increase, and there seem to be many more persons living in towns who cultivate a bit of land in the country as a subsidiary employment.

Taken as a whole the absolute fall off in the number of those working upon the soil is not large. The decline of small country industries is much more considerable. Here another law of industrial motion comes in, the rapid tendency of manufacture towards centralization in the towns, which we have discussed in the last chapter. Here we are concerned only with its effect in stamping out small rural industries. The growth of the railway has been the chief agent in the work. Wherever the railroad has penetrated a country it has withered the ancient cottage industries of our land. It is true that even before the time of railways the development of machinery had in large measure destroyed the spinning and weaving trades, which in Lancashire, Yorkshire, and elsewhere had given employment to large numbers of country families. The railway, and the constant application of new machinery have completed this work of destruction, and have likewise abolished a number of small handicrafts, such as hand-stitched boots, and lace, which flourished in western and midland districts, Nor is this all. The same potent forces have transferred to towns many branches of work connected indirectly with agricultural pursuits; country smiths, brickmakers, sawyers, turners, coopers, wheelwrights, are rapidly vanishing from the face of the country.

§ 5. **Attractions of the Town, Economic and Social.** The concrete form in which the industrial forces, which we have described, appeal to the dull-headed rustic is the attraction of higher wages. An elaborate comparison of towns and country wages is not required. It is enough to say that labourer's wages in London and other large cities are some 50 per cent, higher than the wages of agricultural labourers in most parts of England, and the wages of skilled labour show a similar relation. Besides the actual difficulty of getting agricultural employment in many parts, improved means of knowledge, and of cheap transport, constantly flaunt this offer of higher wages before the eyes of the more discontented among agricultural workers. It is true that if wages are higher in London, the cost of living is also higher, and the conditions of life and work are generally more detrimental to health and happiness; but these drawbacks are more often realized after the fatal step has been taken than before.

Along with the concrete motive of higher wages there come other inherent attractions of town life.

"The contagion of numbers, the sense of something going on, the theatres and music-halls, the brilliantly-lighted streets and busy crowds"[18] have a very powerful effect on the dawning intelligence of the rustic. The growing accessibility of towns brings these temptations within the reach of all. These social attractions probably contain more evil than good, and act with growing force on the restless and reckless among our country population. The tramp and the beggar find more comfort and more gain in the towns. The action of indiscriminate and spasmodic charity, which still prevails in London and other large centres of riches, is responsible in no small measure for the poverty and degradation of city slums.

"The far-reaching advertisement of irresponsible charity acts as a powerful magnet. Whole sections of the population are demoralized, men and women throwing down their work right and left in order to qualify for relief; while the conclusion of the whole matter is intensified congestion of the labour market—angry bitter feeling for the insufficiency of the pittance, or rejection of the claim." So writes Miss Potter of the famous Mansion House Relief Funds.

It is easy to see how the worthless element from our villages, the loafer, the shiftless, the drunkard, the criminal, naturally gravitates towards its proper place as part of the "social wreckage" of our cities. But the size of this element must not be exaggerated. It forms a comparatively small fraction of the whole. Our city criminal, our city loafer, is generally home-grown, and is not supplied directly from the country. If it were true that only the worthless portion of our country population passed into our cities to perish in the struggle for existence, which is so fatal in city life, we should on the whole have reason to congratulate ourselves. But this is not so. The main body of those who pass into city life are in fact the cream of the native population of the country, drawn by advantages chiefly economic. They consist of large numbers of vigorous young men, mostly between the age of twenty and twenty-five, who leave agriculture for manufacture, or move into towns owing to displacement of handicrafts by wholesale manufacture.

§ 6. **Effect of the Change on National Health.**—This decay of country life, however much we may regret it, seems under present industrial conditions inevitable. Nor is it altogether to be regretted or condemned. The movement indisputably represents a certain equalization of advantages economic, educational, and social. The steady workman who moves into the town generally betters himself from the point of view of immediate material advantages.

But in regarding the movement as a whole a much more serious question confronts us. What is the net result upon the physical well-being of the nation of this drafting of the abler and better country folk into the towns? Let the death-rate first testify. In 1902 the death-rate for the whole rural population was

13.7 per 1000, that of the whole urban population 17.8. Now it is not the case that town life is necessarily more unhealthy than country life to any considerable extent. There are well-to-do districts of London, whole boroughs, such as Hampstead, where the death-rate is considerably lower than the ordinary rural rate. The weight of city mortality falls upon the poor.

Careful statistics justify the conclusion that the death-rate of an average poor district in London, Liverpool, or Glasgow, is quite double that of the average country district which is being drained to feed the city. We now see what the growth of town population, and the decay of the country really means. It means in the first place that each year brings a larger proportion of the nation within reach of the higher rate of mortality, by taking them from more healthy and placing them under less healthy conditions. In the case of the lower classes of workers who gravitate to London, it means putting them in a place where the chance of death in a given year is doubled for them. And remember, this higher death-rate is applied not indiscriminately, but to selected subjects. It is the young, healthy, vigorous blood of the country which is exposed to these unhealthy conditions. A pure Londoner of the third generation, that is, one whose grandparents as well as his parents were born in London, is very seldom found. It is certain that nearly all the most effective vital energy given out in London work, physical and intellectual alike, belongs to men whose fathers were country bred, if they were not country born themselves. In kinds of work where pure physical vigour play an important part, this is most strikingly apparent. The following statistics bearing on the London police force were obtained by Mr. Llewellyn Smith in 1888—

	London born.	Country born.	Total.
Metropolitan Police	2,716	10,908	13,624
City "	194	698	892

Railway men, carriers, omnibus-drivers, corn and timber porters, and those in whose work physique tells most, are all largely drawn from the country. Nor is the physical deterioration of city life to be merely measured by death-rates. Many town influences, which do not appreciably affect mortality, distinctly lower the vitality, which must be taken as the physical measure of the value of life. The denizens of city slums not only die twice as fast as their country cousins, but their health and vigour is less during the time they live.

A fair consideration of these facts discloses something much more important than a mere change in social and industrial conditions. Linked with this change we see a deterioration of the physique of the race as a distinct factor in the problem of city poverty. This is no vague speculation, but a strongly-supported hypothesis, which deserves most serious attention. Dr. Ogle, who has done much work in elucidation of this point, sums up in the following striking language—

"The combined effect of this constantly higher mortality in the towns, and of the constant immigration into it of the pick of the rural population, must clearly be a gradual deterioration of the whole, inasmuch as the more energetic and vigorous members of the community are consumed more rapidly than the rest of the population. The system is one which leads to the survival of the unfittest."

Thus the city figures as a mighty vampire, continually sucking the strongest blood of the country to keep up the abnormal supply of energy it has to give out in the excitement of a too fast and unwholesome life. Whether the science of the future may not supply some decentralizing agency, which shall reverse the centralizing force of modern industry, is not a wholly frivolous speculation to suggest. Some sanguine imaginations already foresee the time when those great natural forces, the economical use of which has compelled men and women to crowd into factories in great cities, may be distributable with such ease and cheapness over the whole surface of the land as no longer to require that close local relation which means overcrowding in work and in home life. If science could do this it would confer upon humanity an advantage far less equivocal than that which belongs to the present reign of iron and steam.

§ 7. **The Extent of Foreign Immigration.**—So much for the inflow from the country districts. But there is another inflow which is drawing close attention, the inflow of cheap foreign labour into our towns. Here again we have first to guard against some exaggeration. It is not true that German, Polish, and Russian Jews are coming over in large battalions to steal all the employment of the English working-man, by under-selling him in the labour-market. In the first place, it should be noted that the foreigners of England, as a whole, bear a smaller proportion to the total population than in any other first-class European state. In 1901 the foreigners were 76 in 10,000 of the population; that is a good deal less than one per cent. Our numbers as a nation are not increased by immigration. On the contrary, between 1871 and 1901 we lost considerably by emigration.[19] Even London, the centre of attraction to foreigners, does not contain nearly so large a per-centage of foreigners as any other great capital. The census gave 3 per cent. as the proportion of foreigners, excluding those born in England of foreign parents. Though this figure is perhaps too low, the true proportion cannot be very large. It is not the number, but the distribution and occupation of the foreign immigrants, that make them an object of so much solicitude. The borough of Stepney contains no less than 40 per cent. of the foreign-born population of London, the foreigners increasing from 15,998 in 1881 to 54,310 in 1901. At present 182 out of every 1000 in this district are foreigners. The proportion is also very high in Holborn, Westminster, Marylebone, Bethnal Green, and St Pancras. The Report of the Royal Commission on Alien Immigration, 1902, states "that the greatest evils produced by the Alien Immigrants here are the overcrowding caused by them in certain districts of London, and the consequent displacement of the native population." The concentration of the immigrant question is attested by the fact that in 1901 no less than 48 per cent. of the total foreign population were resident in six metropolitan boroughs, and in the three cities of Manchester, Liverpool, and Leeds. While a considerable number of them are Germans, French, and Italians, attracted here by better industrial conditions in trades for which they have some special aptitude, a greatly increasing proportion are Russian and Polish Jews, driven to immigrate partly by political and religious persecution, partly for industrial ends, and feeding the unskilled labour-market in certain manufactures of our great cities.

§ 8. **The Jew as an Industrial Competitor.**—Looking at these foreigners as individuals, there is much to be said in their favour. They do not introduce a lower morality into the quarters where they settle, as the Chinese are said to do; nor are they quarrelsome and law-breaking, like the low-class Italians who swarm into America. Their habits, so far as cleanliness is concerned, are perhaps not desirable, but the standard of the native population of Whitechapel is not sensitively high. For the most part, and this is true especially of the Jews, they are steady, industrious, quiet, sober, thrifty, quick to learn, and tolerably honest. From the point of view of the old Political Economy, they are the very people to be encouraged, for they turn out the largest quantity of wealth at the lowest cost of production. If it is the chief end for a nation to accumulate the largest possible stock of material wealth, it is evident that these are the very people we require to enable us to achieve our object.

But if we consider it is sound national policy to pay regard to the welfare of all classes engaged in producing this wealth, we may regard this foreign immigration in quite another light. The very virtues just enumerated are the chief faults we have to find with the foreign Jew. Just because he is willing and able to work so hard for so little pay, willing to undertake any kind of work out of which he can make a living, because he can surpass in skill, industry, and adaptability the native Londoner, the foreign Jew is such a terrible competitor. He is the nearest approach to the ideal "economic" man, the "fittest" person to survive in trade competition. Admirable in domestic morality, and an orderly citizen, he is almost void of social morality. No compunction or consideration for his fellow-worker will keep him from underselling and overreaching them; he acquires a thorough mastery of all the dishonourable tricks of trade which are difficult to restrain by law; the superior calculating intellect, which is a national heritage, is used unsparingly to enable him to take advantage of every weakness, folly, and vice of the society in which he lives.

§ 9. **Effect of Foreign Competition.**—One other quality he has in common with the mass of poor foreigners who compete in the London labour market—he can live on less than the Englishman. What Mrs Webb says of the Polish Jew, is in large measure true of all cheap foreign labour—"As industrial competitor, the Polish Jew is fettered by no definite standard of life; it rises and falls with his opportunities; he is not depressed by penury, and he is not demoralized by gain." The fatal significance of this is evident. We have seen that notwithstanding a general rise in the standard of comfort of the mass of labourers, there still remains in all our cities a body of labouring men and women engaged in doing ill-paid and irregular work for wages which keep them always on the verge of starvation. Now consider what it means for these people to have brought into their midst a number of competitors who can live even more cheaply than they can live, and who will consent to toil from morning to night for whatever they can get. These new-comers are obviously able, in their eagerness for work, to drive down the rate of wages even below what represents starvation-point for the native worker. The insistence of the poorer working-classes, under the stimulus of new-felt wants, the growing enlightenment of public opinion, have slowly and gradually won, even for the poorer workers in English cities, some small advance in material comfort, some slight expansion in the meaning of the term "necessaries of life." Turn a few shiploads of Polish Jews upon any of these districts, and they will and must in the struggle for life destroy the whole of this. Remember it is not merely the struggle of too many workers competing on equal terms for an insufficient quantity of work. That is terrible enough. But when the struggle is between those accustomed to a higher, and those accustomed to a lower, standard of life, the latter can obviously oust the former, and take their work. Just as a base currency drives out of circulation a pure currency, so does a lower standard of comfort drive out a higher one. This is the vital question regarding foreign immigration which has to be faced.

Nor is it merely a question of the number of these foreigners. The inflow of a comparatively small number into a neighbourhood where much of the work is low-skilled and irregular, will often produce an effect which seems quite out of proportion to the actual number of the invaders. Where work is slack and difficult to get, a very small addition of low-living foreigners will cause a perceptible fall in the entire wages of the neighbourhood in the employments which their competition affects. It is true that the Jew does not remain a low-skilled labourer for starvation wages. Beginning at the bottom of the ladder, he rises by his industry and skill, until he gets into the rank of skilled workers, or more frequently becomes a sub-contractor, or a small shopkeeper. It might appear that as he thus rose, the effect of his competition in the low skilled labour market would disappear. And this would be so were it not for the persistent arrival of new-comers to take the place of those who rise. It is the continuity in the flow of foreign emigration which constitutes the real danger.

Economic considerations do not justify us in expecting any speedy check upon this flow. The growing means of communication among nations, the cheapening of transport, the breaking down of international prejudices, must, if they are left free to operate, induce the labourer to seek the best market for his labour, and thus tend to equalize the condition of labour in the various communities, raising the level of the lower paid and lower lived at the expense of the higher paid and higher lived.

§ 10. The Water-tight Compartment Theory.—One point remains to be mentioned. It is sometimes urged that the foreign Jews who come to our shores do not injure our low skilled workers to any considerable extent, because they do not often enter native trades, but introduce new trades which would not have existed at all were it not for their presence. They work, it is said, in water-tight compartments, competing among themselves, but not directly competing with English workers. Now if it were the case that these foreigners really introduced new branches of production designed to stimulate and supply new wants this contention would have much weight. The Flemings who in Edward III.'s reign introduced the finer kinds of weaving into England, and the Huguenot refugees who established new branches of the silk, glass, and paper manufactures, conferred a direct service upon English commerce, and their presence in the labour market was probably an indirect service to the English workers. But this is not the case with the modern Jew immigrants. They have not stimulated or supplied new wants. It is not even correct to say that most of them do not directly compete with native labour. It is true that certain branches of the cheap clothing trade have been their creation. The cheap coat trade, which they almost monopolize, seems due to their presence. But even here they have established no new *kind* of trade. To their cheap labour perhaps is due in some cases the large export trade in cheap clothing, but even then it is doubtful whether the work would not otherwise have been done by machinery under healthier conditions, and have furnished work and wages for English workers. During the last decade they have been entering more and more into direct competition with British labour in the cabinet-making, shoemaking, baking, hair-dressing, and domestic service occupations. Lastly, they enter into direct competition of the worst form with English female labour, which is driven in these very clothing trades to accept work and wages which are even too low to tempt the Jews of Whitechapel. The constant infiltration of cheap immigrant labour is in large measure responsible for the existence of the "sweating workshops," and the survival of low forms of industrial development which form a factor in the problem of poverty.

CHAPTER IV.

"THE SWEATING SYSTEM."

§ 1. Origin of the Term "Sweating."—Having gained insight into some of the leading industrial forces of the age, we can approach more hopefully the study of that aspect of City poverty, commonly known as the "Sweating System."

The first thing is to get a definite meaning to the term. Since the examination of experts before the recent "Lords' Committee" elicited more than twenty widely divergent definitions of this "Sweating System," some care is required at the outset of our inquiry. The common use of the term "Sweating System" is itself responsible for much ambiguity, for the term "system" presupposes a more or less distinct form of organization of industry identified with the evils of sweating. Now as it should be one of the objects of inquiry to ascertain whether there exists any one such definite form, it will be better at the outset to confine ourselves to the question, "What is Sweating?"

As an industrial term the word seems to have been first used among journeymen tailors. The tailoring houses which once executed all orders on their own premises, by degrees came to recognize the convenience of giving out work to tailors who would work at their own homes. The long hours which the home workers were induced to work in order to increase their pay, caused the term "Sweater" to be applied to them by the men who worked for fixed hours on the tailors' premises, and who found their work passing more and more into the hands of the home workers. Thus we learn that originally it was long hours and not low wages which constituted "sweating." School-boy slang still uses the word in this same sense. Moreover, the first sweater was one who "sweated" himself, not others. But soon when more and more tailoring work was "put out," the home worker, finding he could undertake more than he could execute, employed his family and also outsiders to help him. This makes the second stage in the evolution of the term; the sweater now "sweated" others as well as himself, and he figured as a "middleman" between the tailoring firm which employed him, and the assistants whom he employed for fixed wages. Other clothing trades have passed through the same process of development, and have produced a sub-contracting middleman. The term "sweater" has thus by the outside world, and sometimes by the workers themselves, come to be generally applied to sub-contractors in small City trades. But the fact of the special application has not prevented the growth of a wider signification of "sweating" and "sweater." As the long hours worked in the tailors' garrets were attended with other evils—a low rate of wages, unsanitary conditions, irregularity of employment, and occasional tyranny in all the forms which attend industrial authority—all these evils became attached to the notion of sweating. The word has thus grown into a generic term to express this disease of City poverty from its purely industrial side. Though "long hours" was the gist of the original complaint, low wages have come to be recognized as equally belonging to the essence of "sweating." In some cases, indeed, low wages have become the leading idea, so that employers are classed as sweaters who pay low wages, without consideration of hours or other conditions of employment. Trade Unions, for example, use the term "sweating" specifically to express the conduct of employers who pay less than the "standard" rate of wages. The abominable sanitary condition of many of the small workshops, or private dwellings of workers, is to many reformers the most essential element in sweating.

§ 2. **Present Applications of the Name.**—When the connotation of the term "sweating" had become extended so as to include along with excessive hours of labour, low wages, unsanitary conditions of work, and other evils, which commonly belong to the method of sub-contract employment, it was only natural that the same word should come to be applied to the same evils when they were found outside the sub-contract system. For though it has been, and still is, true, that where the method of sub-contract is used the workers are frequently "sweated," and though to the popular mind the sub-contractor still figures as the typical sweater, it is not right to regard "sub-contract" as the real cause of sweating. For it is found—

Firstly, that in some trades sub-contract is used without the evils of sweating being present. Mr. Burnett, labour correspondent to the Board of Trade, in his evidence before the Lords' Committee, maintains that where Trade Unions are strong, as in the engineering trade, sub-contract is sometimes employed under conditions which are entirely "unobjectionable." So too in the building trades, sub-contract is not always attended by "sweating."

Secondly, much of the worst "sweating" is found where the element of sub-contract is entirely wanting, and where there is no trace of a ravenous middleman. This will be found especially in women's employments. Miss Potter, after a close investigation of this point, arrives at the conclusion that "undoubtedly the worst paid work is made under the direction of East End retail slop-shops, or for tally-men—a business from which contact, even in the equivocal form of wholesale trading, has been eliminated."[20] The term "sweating" must be deemed as applicable to the case of the women employed in the large steam-laundries, who on Friday and Saturday work for fifteen or sixteen hours a day, to the overworked and under-paid waitresses in restaurants and shops, to the men who, as Mr. Burleigh testified, "are employed in some of the wealthiest houses of business, and received for an average working week of ninety-five hours, board, lodging, and £15 a year," as it is to the tailoress who works fourteen hours a day for Whitechapel sub-contractors.

The terms "sweating" and "sweating System," then, after

originating in a narrow application to the practice of over-work under sub-contractors in the lower branches of the tailoring trade, has expanded into a large generic term, to express the condition of all overworked, ill-paid, badly-housed workers in our cities. It sums up the industrial or economic aspects of the problem of city poverty. Scarcely any trade in its lowest grades is free from it; in nearly all we find the wretched "fag end" where the workers are miserably oppressed. This is true not only of the poorest manual labour, that of the sandwich-man, with his wage of 1s. 2d. per diem, and of the lowest class of each manufacturing trade in East and Central London. It is true of the relatively unskilled labour in every form of employment; the miserable writing-clerk, who on 25s. a week or less has to support a wife and children and an appearance of respectability; the usher, who grinds out low-class instruction through the whole tedious day for less than the wage of a plain cook; the condition of these and many other kinds of low-class brain-workers is only a shade less pitiable than the "sweating" of manual labourers, and the causes, as we shall see, are much the same. If our investigation of "sweating" is chiefly confined to the condition of the manual labourer, it is only because the malady there touches more directly and obviously the prime conditions of physical life, not because the nature of the industrial disease is different.

§ 3. Leading "Sweating" Trades.—It is next desirable to have some clear knowledge of the particular trades in which the worst forms of "sweating" are found, and the extent to which it prevails in each. The following brief summary is in a large measure drawn from evidence furnished to the recent Lords' Committee on the Sweating System. Since the sweating in women's industries is so important a subject as to demand a separate treatment, the facts stated here will chiefly apply to male industries.

Tailoring.—In the tailoring trade the best kind of clothes are still made by highly-skilled and well-paid workmen, but the bulk of the cheap clothing is in the hands of "sweaters," who are sometimes skilled tailors, sometimes not, and who superintend the work of cheap unskilled hands. In London the coat trade should be distinguished from the vest and trousers trade. The coat-making trade in East London is a closely-defined district, with an area of one square mile, including the whole of Whitechapel and parts of two adjoining parishes. The trade is almost entirely in the hands of Jews, who number from thirty to forty thousand persons. Recent investigations disclosed 906 workshops, which, in the quality and conditions of the work done in them, may be graded according to the number of hands employed. The larger workshops, employing from ten to twenty-five hands or more, generally pay fair wages, and are free from symptoms of sweating. But in the small workshops, which form about 80 per cent of the whole number, the common evils of the sweating system assert themselves—overcrowding, bad sanitation, and excessive hours of labour. Thirteen and fourteen hours are the nominal day's work for men; and those workshops which do not escape the Factory Inspector assign a nominal factory day for women; but "among the imperfectly taught workers in the slop and stock trade, and more especially in the domestic workshops, under-pressers, plain machinists, and fellers are in many instances expected to 'convenience' their masters, i.e. to work for twelve or fifteen hours in return for ten or thirteen hours' wage."[21] The better class workers, who require some skill, get comparatively high wages even in the smaller workshops, though the work is irregular; but the general hands engaged in making 1s. coats, generally women, get a maximum of *1s. 6d.*, and a minimum which is indefinitely below 1s. for a twelve hours' day. This low-class work is also hopeless. The raw hand, or "greener" as he is called, will often work through his apprenticeship for nominal wages; but he has the prospect of becoming a machinist, and earning from 6s. to 10s. a day, or of becoming in his turn a sweater. The general hand has no such hope. The lowest kind of coat-making, however, is refused by the Jew contractor, and falls to Gentile women. These women also undertake most of the low-class vest and trousers making, generally take their work direct from a wholesale house, and execute it at home, or in small workshops. The price for this work is miserably low, partly by reason of the competition of provincial factories, partly for reasons to be discussed in a later chapter. Women will work for twelve or fifteen hours a day throughout the week as "trousers finishers," for a net-earning of as little as 4s. or 5s. Such is the condition of inferior unskilled labour in the tailoring trade. It should however be understood that in "tailoring," as in other "sweating" trades, the lowest figures quoted must be received with caution. The wages of a "greener," a beginner or apprentice, should not be taken as evidence of a low wage in the trade, for though it is a lamentable thing that the learner should have to live upon the value of his prentice work, it is evident that under no commercial condition could he support himself in comfort during this period. It is the normal starvation wage of the low-class experienced hand which is the true measure of "sweating" in these trades. Two facts serve to give prominence to the growth of "sweating" in the tailoring trades. During the last few years there has been a fall of some 30 per cent, in the prices paid for the same class of work. During the same period the irregularity of work has increased. Even in fairly large shops the work for ordinary labour only averages some three days in the week, while we must reckon two and a half days for unskilled workers in smaller workshops, or working at home.

Among provincial towns Liverpool, Manchester, and Leeds show a rapid growth of sweating in the clothing trade. In each case the evil is imputed to "an influx of foreigners, chiefly Jews." In each town the same conditions appear—irregular work and wages, unsanitary conditions, over-crowding, evasion of inspection. The growth in Leeds is remarkable. "There are now ninety-seven Jewish workshops in the city, whereas five years ago there were scarcely a dozen. The number of Jews engaged in the tailoring trade is about three thousand. The whole Jewish population of Leeds is about five thousand."[22]

Boot-making.—The hand-sewn trade, which constitutes the

upper stratum of this industry, is executed for the most part by skilled workers, who get good wages for somewhat irregular employment. There are several strong trade organizations, and though the hours are long, extending occasionally to thirteen or fourteen hours, the worst forms of sweating are not found. So too in the upper branches of machine-sewn boots, the skilled hands get fairly high wages. But the lower grades of machine-made boots, and the "sew-rounds," i.e. fancy shoes and slippers, which form a large part of the industry in London, present some of the worst features of the "sweating system." The "sweating master" plays a large part here. "In a busy week a comparatively competent 'sweater' may earn from 18s. to 25s. less skilful hands may get 15s. or 16s. but boys and newly-arrived foreigners take 10s., 8s., 7s., or less; while the masters, after paying all expenses, would, according to their own estimates, make not less than 30s., and must, in many cases, net much higher sums. Owing, however, to the irregularity of their employment, the average weekly earnings of both masters and men throughout the year fall very greatly below the amount which they can earn when in full work."[23] For the lowest kinds of work an ordinary male hand appears to be able to earn not more than 15s. per week. A slow worker, it is said, would earn an average of some 10s. to 12s. per week. The hours of labour for sweating work appear to be from fifteen to eighteen per diem, and "greeners" not infrequently work eighteen to twenty hours a day. Women, who are largely used in making "felt and carpet uppers," cannot, if they work their hardest, make more than 1s. 3d. a day. In the lowest class of work wages fall even lower. Mr. Schloss gives the wages of five men working in a small workshop, whose average is less than 11s. a week. These wages do not of course represent skilled work at all. Machinery has taken over all the skilled work, and left a dull laborious monotony of operations which a very few weeks' practice enable a completely unskilled worker to undertake. Probably the bulk of the cheapest work is executed by foreigners, although from figures taken in 1887, of four typical London parishes, it appeared that only 16 per cent, of the whole trade were foreigners. In the lower classes of goods a considerable fall of price has occurred during the fast few years, and perhaps the most degraded conditions of male labour are to be found in the boot trade. A large proportion of the work throughout the trade is out-work, and therefore escapes the operation of the Factory Act. The competition among small employers is greatly accentuated by the existence of a form of middleman known as the "factor," who is an agent who gets his profit by playing off one small manufacturer against another, keeping down prices, and consequently wages, to a minimum. A large number of the small producers are extremely poor, and owing to the System which enables them to obtain material from leather-merchants on short credit, are constantly obliged to sell at a disadvantage to meet their bills. The "factor," as a speculator, takes advantage of this to accumulate large stocks at low prices, and throwing them on the market in large quantities when wholesale prices rise, causes much irregularity in the trade.

The following quotation from the Report of the Lords' Committee sums up the chief industrial forces which are at work, and likewise illustrates the confusion of causes with symptoms, and casual concomitants, which marks the "common sense" investigations of intricate social phenomena. "It will be seen from the foregoing epitome of the evidence, that sweating in the boot trade is mainly traced by the witnesses to the introduction of machinery, and a more complete system of subdivision of labour, coupled with immigration from abroad and foreign competition. Some witnesses have traced it in a great measure, if not principally, to the action of factors; some to excessive competition among small masters as well as men; others have accused the Trades Unions of a course of action which has defeated the end they have in view, namely, effectual combination, by driving work, owing to their arbitrary conduct, out of the factory into the house of the worker, and of handicapping England in the race with foreign countries, by setting their faces against the use of the best machinery."[24]

Shirt-making.—Perhaps no other branch of the clothing trade shows so large an area of utter misery as shirt-making, which is carried on, chiefly by women, in East London. The complete absence of adequate organization, arising from the fact that the work is entirely out-work, done not even by clusters of women in workshops, but almost altogether by scattered workers in their own homes, makes this perhaps the completest example of the evils of sweating. The commoner shirts are sold wholesale at 10s. 6d. per dozen. Of this sum, it appears that the worker gets 2s. 1½d., and the sweater sometimes as much as 4s. The competition of married women enters here, for shirt-making requires little skill and no capital; hence it can be undertaken, and often is, by married women, anxious to increase the little and irregular earnings of their husbands, and willing to work all day for whatever they can get. Some of the worst cases brought before the Lords' Committee showed that a week's work of this kind brings in a net gain of from 3s. to 5s. It appears likely that few unmarried women or widows can undertake this work, because it does not suffice to afford a subsistence wage. But if this is so, it must be remembered that the competition of married women has succeeded in underselling the unmarried women, who might otherwise have been able to obtain this work at a wage which would have supported life. The fact that those who work at shirt-making do not depend entirely on it for a livelihood, is an aggravation rather than an extenuation of the sweating character of this employment.

§ 4. Some minor "Sweating" Trades.—Mantle-making is also a woman's industry. The wages are just sufficiently higher than in shirt-making to admit the introduction of the lowest grades of unsupported female workers. From 1s. 3d. to 1s. 6d. a day can be made at this work.

Furring employs large numbers of foreign males, and some thousands of both native and foreign females. It is almost entirely conducted in small workshops, under the conduct of middlemen, who receive the expensive furs from manufacturers, and hire "hands" to sew and work them up. Wages have fallen during the last few years to the barest subsistence point, and even below. Wages for men are put at 10s. or 12s., and in the case of girls and young women, fall as low as 4s.; a sum which is in itself insufficient to support life, and must therefore be only paid to women and girls who are partly subsisted by the efforts of relatives with whom they live, or by the wages of vice.

In cabinet-making and upholstery, the same disintegrating influences have been at work which we noted in tailoring. Many firms which formerly executed all orders on their own premises, now buy from small factors, and much of the lowest and least skilled work is undertaken by small "garret-masters," or even by single workmen who hawk round their wares for sale on their own account. The higher and skilled branches are protected by trade organizations, and there is no evidence that wages have fallen; but in the less skilled work, owing perhaps in part to the competition of machinery, prices have fallen, and wages are low. There is evidence that the sub-contract system here is sometimes carried through several stages, much to the detriment of the workman who actually executes the orders.

One of the most degraded among the sweating industries in the country is chain and nail-making. The condition of the chain-makers of Cradley Heath has called forth much public attention. The system of employment is a somewhat complicated one. A middleman, called a "fogger," acts as a go-between, receiving the material from the master, distributing it among the workers, and collecting the finished product. Evidence before the Committee shows that an accumulation of intricate forms of abuse of power existed, including in some cases systematic evasion of the Truck Act. Much of the work is extremely laborious, hours are long, twelve hours forming an ordinary day, and the wage paid is the barest subsistence wage. Much of the work done by women is quite unfit for them.

§ 5. Who is the Sweater? The Sub-contractor?—These facts relating to a few of the principal trades in the lower branches of which "sweating" thrives, must suffice as a general indication of the character of the disease as it infests the inferior strata of almost all industries.

Having learnt what "sweating" means, our next question naturally takes the form, Who is the sweater? Who is the person responsible for this state of things? John Bull is concrete, materialistic in his feeling and his reasoning. He wants to find an individual, or a class embodiment of sweating. If he can find the sweater, he is prepared to loathe and abolish him. Our indignation and humanitarianism requires a scape-goat. As we saw, many of the cases of sweating were found where there was a sub-contractor. To our hasty vision, here seems to be the responsible party. Forty years ago *Alton Locke* gave us a powerful picture of the wicked sub-contracting tailor, who, spider-like, lured into his web the unfortunate victim, and sucked his blood for gain. The indignation of tender-hearted but loose-thinking philanthropists, short-visioned working-class orators, assisted by the satire of the comic journal, has firmly planted in the imagination of the public an ideal of an East London sweater; an idle, bloated middleman, whose expansive waistcoat is decorated with resplendent seals and watch-chains, who drinks his Champagne, and smokes his perfumed cigar, as he watches complacently the sunken faces and cowering forms of the wretched creatures whose happiness, health, and very life are sacrificed to his heartless greed.

Now a fair study of facts show this creature to be little else than a myth. The miseries of the sweating den are no exaggeration, they are attested by a thousand reliable witnesses; but this monster human spider is not found there. Though opinions differ considerably as to the precise status of the sweating middleman, it is evident that in the worst "sweating" trades he is not idle, and he is not rich. In cases where the well-to-do, comfortable sub-contractor is found, he generally pays fair wages, and does not grossly abuse his power. When the worst features of sweating are present, the master sweater is nearly always poor, his profits driven down by competition, so that he barely makes a living. It is, indeed, evident that in many of the worst Whitechapel sweating-dens the master does not on the average make a larger income than the more highly paid of his machinists. So, too, most of these "sweaters" work along with their hands, and work just as hard. Some, indeed, have represented this sweating middleman as one who thrusts himself between the proper employer and the working man in order to make a gain for himself without performing any service. But the bulk of evidence goes to show that the sweater, even when he does not occupy himself in detailed manual labour, performs a useful work of superintendence and management. "The sweater in the vast majority of cases is the one man in the workshop who can, and does, perform each and any branch of the trade."

For the old adage, which made a tailor the ninth part of a man, has been completely reversed by the subdivision of work in modern industry. It now takes more than nine men to make a tailor. We have foremen or cutters, basters, machinists, fellers, button-holers, pressers, general workers, &c. No fewer than twenty-five such subdivisions have been marked in the trade. Since the so-called tailor is no tailor at all, but a "button-holer" or "baster," it is obvious that the working of such a system requires some one capable of general direction.

This opinion is not, however, inconsistent with the belief that such work of "direction" or "organization" may be paid on a scale wholly out of proportion to the real worth of the services performed. Extremely strong evidence has been tendered to show that in many large towns, especially in Leeds and Liverpool, the "sweating" tailor has frequently "no practical knowledge of his trade." The ignorance and incompetence of the working tailors enables a Jew with a business mind, by bribing managers, to obtain a contract for work which he makes no pretence to execute himself. His ability consists simply in the fact that he can get more work at a cheaper rate out of the poorer workmen than the manager of a large firm. In his capacity of middleman he is a "convenience," and for his work, which is nominally that of master tailor, really that of sweating manager, he gets his pay.

Part of the "service" thus rendered by the sweater is doubtless that he acts as a screen to the employing firm. Public opinion, and "the reputation of the firm," would not permit a well-known business to employ the workers *directly* under their own roof upon the terms which the secrecy of the sweater's den enables them to pay. But in spite of this, whether the "Jew sweater" is really a competent tailor or is a mere "organizer" of poor labour, it should be distinctly understood that he is paid for the performance of real work, which under the present industrial system has a use.

§ 6. Different Species of Middlemen.—It may be well here to say something on the general position of the "middleman" in commerce. The popular notion that the "middleman" is a useless being, and that if he could be abolished all would go well, arises from a confusion of thought which deserves notice. This confusion springs from a failure to understand that the "middleman" is a part of a commercial System. He is not a mere intruder, a parasitic party, who forces his way between employer and worker, or between producer and consumer, and without conferring any service, extracts for himself a profit which involves a loss to the worker or the consumer, or to both. If we examine this notion, either by reference to facts, or from *à priori* consideration, we shall find it based on a superstition. "Middleman" is a broad generic term used to describe a man through whose hands goods pass on their way to the consuming public, but who does not appear to add any value to the goods he handles. At any stage in the production of these goods, previous to their final distribution, the middleman may come in and take his profit for no visible work done. He may be a speculator, buying up grain or timber, and holding or manipulating it in the large markets; or he may be a wholesale merchant, who, buying directly from the fisherman, and selling to the retail fishmonger, is supposed to be responsible for the high price of fish; he may be the retailer who in East London is supposed to cause the high price of vegetables.

With these species of middlemen we are not now concerned, except to say that their work, which is that of distribution, i.e. the more convenient disposal of forms of material wealth, may be equally important with the work of the farmer, the fisherman, or the market-gardener, though the latter produce changes in the shape and appearance of the goods, while the former do not. The middleman who stands between the employing firm and the worker is of three forms. He may undertake a piece of work for a wholesale house, and taking the material home, execute it with the aid of his family or outside assistants. This is the chamber-master proper, or "sweater" in the tailoring trade. Or he may act as distributor, receive the material, and undertake to find workers who will execute it at their own homes, he undertaking the responsibility of collection. Where the workers are scattered over a large city area, or over a number of villages, this work of distribution, and its responsibility, may be considerable. Lastly, there may be the "sub-contractor" proper, who undertakes to do a portion of a work already contracted for, and either finds materials and tools, and pays workers to work for him, or sublets parts of his contract to workers who provide their own materials and tools. The mining and building trades contain various examples of such sub-contracts. Now in none of these cases is the middleman a mere parasite. In every case he does work, which, though as a rule it does not alter the material form of the goods with which it deals, adds distinct value to them, and is under present industrial conditions equally necessary, and equally entitled to fair remuneration with the work of the other producers. The old maxim "nihil ex nihilo fit" is as true in commerce as in chemistry. In a competitive society a man can get nothing for nothing. If the middleman is a capitalist he may get something for use of his capital; but that too implies that his capital is put to some useful work.

§ 7. **Work and Pay of the Middleman.**—The complaint that

the middleman confers no service, and deserves no pay, is the result of two fallacies. The first, to which allusion has been made already, consists in the failure to recognize the work of distribution done by the middleman. The second and more important is the confusion of mind which leads people to conclude that because under different circumstances a particular class of work might be dispensed with, therefore that work is under present circumstances useless and undeserving of reward. Lawyers might be useless if there were no dishonesty or crime, but we do not therefore feel justified in describing as useless the present work they do. With every progress of new inventions we are constantly rendering useless some class or other of undoubted "workers." So the middleman in his various capacities may be dispensed with, if the organization of industrial society is so changed that he is no longer required; but until such changes are affected he must get, and deserves, his pay. It may indeed be true that certain classes of middlemen are enabled by the position they hold to extract either from their employers or from the public a profit which seems out of proportion to the services they render. But this is by no means generally the case with the middleman in his capacity of "sweater." Even where a middleman does make large profits, we are not justified in describing such gain as excessive or unfair, unless we are prepared to challenge the claim of "free competition" to determine the respective money values of industrial services. The "sweating" middleman does work which is at present necessary; he gets pay; if we think he gets too much, are we prepared with any rule to determine even approximately how much he ought to get?

§ 8. **The Employer as "Sweater."**—Since it appears that the middleman often sweats others of necessity because he is himself "sweated," in the low terms of the contract he makes, and since much of the worst "sweating" takes place where firms of employers deal directly with the "workers," it may seem that the blame is shifted on to the employer, and that the real responsibility rests with him. Now is this so? When we see an important firm representing a large capital and employing many hands, paying a wage barely sufficient for the maintenance of life, we are apt to accuse the employers of meanness and extortion: we say this firm could afford to pay higher wages, but they prefer to take higher profits; the necessity of the poor is their opportunity. Now this accusation ought to be fairly faced. It will then be found to fall with very different force according as it is addressed to one or other of two classes of employers. Firms which are shielded from the full force of the competition of capital by the possession of some patent or trade secret, some special advantage in natural resources, locality, or command of markets, are generally in a position which will enable them to reap a rate of profit, the excess of which beyond the ordinary rate of profit measures the value of the practical monopoly they possess. The owners of a coal-mine, or a gas-works, a special brand of soap or biscuits, or a ring of capitalists who have secured control of a market, are often able to pay wages above the market level without endangering their commercial position. Even in a trade like the Lancashire cotton trade, where there is free competition among the various firms, a rapid change in the produce market may often raise the profits of the trade, so that all or nearly all the employing firms could afford to pay higher wages without running any risk of failure. Now employers who are in a position like this are morally responsible for the hardship and degradation they inflict if they pay wages insufficient for decent maintenance. Their excuse that they are paying the market rate of wages, and that if their men do not choose to work for this rate there are plenty of others who will, is no exoneration of their conduct unless it be distinctly admitted that "moral considerations" have no place in commerce. Employers who in the enjoyment of this superior position pay bare subsistence wages, and defend themselves by the plea that they pay the "market rate," are "sweaters," and the blame of sweating will rightly attach to them.

But this is not to be regarded as the normal position of employers. Among firms unsheltered by a monopoly, and exposed to the full force of capitalist competition, the rate of profit is also at "the minimum of subsistence," that is to say, if higher wages were paid to the employés, the rate of profit would either become a negative quantity, or would be so low that capital could no longer be obtained for investment in such a trade. Generally it may be said that a joint-stock company and a private firm, trading as most firms do chiefly on borrowed capital, could not pay higher wages and stand its ground in the competition with other firms. If a benevolent employer engaged in a manufacture exposed to open competition undertook to raise the wages of his men twenty per cent, in order to lift them to a level of comfort which satisfied his benevolence, he must first sacrifice the whole of his "wage of superintendence," and he will then find that he can only pay the necessary interest on his borrowed capital out of his own pocket: in fact he would find he had essayed to do what in the long run was impossible. The individual employer under normal circumstances is no more to blame for the low wages, long hours, &c., than is the middleman. He could not greatly improve the industrial condition of his employés, however much he might wish.

§ 9. The Purchaser as "Sweater." A third view, a little longer-sighted than the others, casts the blame upon the purchasing public. Wages must be low, we are told, because the purchaser insists on low prices. It is the rage for "cheapness" which is the real cause, according to this line of thought. Formerly the customer was content to pay a fair price for an article to a tradesman with whom he dealt regularly, and whose interest it was to sell him a fair article. The tradesman could thus afford to pay the manufacturer a price which would enable him to pay decent wages, and in return for this price he insisted upon good work being put into the goods he bought. Thus there was no demand for bad work. Skilled work alone could find a market, and skilled work requires the payment of decent wages. The growth of modern competition has changed all this. Regular custom has given way to touting and advertising, the bond of interest between consumer and shopkeeper is broken, the latter seeks merely to sell the largest quantity of wares to any one who will buy, the former to pay the lowest price to any one who will sell him what he thinks he wants. Hence a deterioration in the quality of many goods. It is no longer the interest of many tradesmen to sell sound wares; the consumer can no longer rely upon the recommendation of the retailer as a skilled judge of the quality of a particular line of goods; he is thrown back upon his own discrimination, and as an amateur he is apt to be worsted in a bargain with a specialist. There is no reason to suppose that customers are meaner than they used to be. They always bought things as cheaply as they knew how to get them. The real point is that they are less able to detect false cheapness than they used to be. Not merely do they no longer rely upon a known and trusted retailer to protect them from the deceits of the manufacturer, but the facilities for deception are continually increasing. The greater complexity of trade, the larger variety of commodities, the increased specialization in production and distribution, the growth of "a science of adulteration" have immensely increased the advantage which the professional salesman possesses over the amateur customer. Hence the growth of goods meant not for use but for sale—jerry-built houses, adulterated food, sham cloth and leather, botched work of every sort, designed merely to pass muster in a hurried act of sale. To such a degree of refinement have the arts of deception been carried that the customer is liable to be tricked and duped at every turn. It is not that he foolishly prefers to buy a bad article at a low price, but that he cannot rely upon his judgment to discriminate good from bad quality; he therefore prefers to pay a low price because he has no guarantee that by paying more he will get a better article. It is this fact, and not a mania for cheapness, which explains the flooding of the market with bad qualities of wares. This effectual demand for bad workmanship on the part of the consuming public is no doubt directly responsible for many of the worst phases of "sweating." Slop clothes and cheap boots are turned out in large quantities by workers who have no claim to be called tailors or shoemakers. A few weeks' practice suffices to furnish the quantum of clumsy skill or deceit required for this work. That is to say, the whole field of unskilled labour is a recruiting-ground for the "sweater" or small employer in these and other clothing trades. If the public insisted on buying good articles, and paid the price requisite for their production, these "sweating" trades would be impossible. But before we saddle the consuming public with the blame, we must bear in mind the following extenuating circumstances.

§ 10. **What the Purchaser can do.**—The payment of a higher price is no guarantee that the workers who produce the goods are not "sweated." If I am competent to discriminate well-made goods from badly-made goods, I shall find it to my interest to abstain from purchasing the latter, and shall be likewise doing what I can to discourage "sweating." But by merely paying a higher price for goods of the same quality as those which I could buy at a lower price, I may be only putting a larger profit in the hands of the employers of this low-skilled labour, and am certainly doing nothing to decrease that demand for badly-made goods which appears to be the root of the evil. The purchaser who wishes to discourage sweating should look first to the quality of the goods he buys, rather than to the price. Skilled labour is seldom sweated to the same degree as unskilled labour, and a high class of workmanship will generally be a guarantee of decent wages. In so far as the purchaser lacks ability to accurately gauge quality, he has little security that by paying a higher price he is securing better wages for the workers. The so-called respectability of a well-known house is a poor guarantee that its employés are getting decent wages, and no guarantee at all that the workers in the various factories with which the firm deals are well paid. It is impossible for a private customer to know that by dealing with a given shop he is not directly or indirectly encouraging "sweating." It might, however, be feasible for the consuming public to appoint committees, whose special work it should be to ascertain that goods offered in shops were produced by firms who paid decent wages. If a "white list" of firms who paid good wages, and dealt only with manufacturers who paid good wages, were formed, purchasers who desired to discourage sweating would be able to feel a certain security, so far, at any rate, as the later stages of production are concerned, which ordinary knowledge of the world and business will not at present enable them to obtain. The force of an organized public opinion, even that of a respectable minority, brought to bear upon notorious "sweating" firms, would doubtless be of great avail, if carefully applied.

At the same time, it must not for a moment be imagined that the problem of poverty would be solved if we could insure, by the payment of higher prices for better qualities of goods, the extermination of the sweating trades. This low, degraded and degrading work enables large numbers of poor inefficient workers to eke out a bare subsistence. If it were taken away, the direct result would be an accession of poverty and misery. The demand for skilled labour would be greater, but the unskilled labourer cannot pass the barrier and compete for this; the overflow of helpless, hopeless, feeble, unskilled labour would be greater than ever. Whatever the ultimate effects of decreasing the demand for unskilled labour might be, the misery of the immediate effects could not be lightly set aside. This contradiction of the present certain effect and the probable future effects confronts the philanthropist at every turn. The condition of the London match-girls may serve as an illustration of this. Their miserable life has rightly roused the indignation of all kind-hearted people. The wretched earnings they take have provoked people to suggest that we should put an end to the trade by refusing to buy from them. But since the earnings of these girls depend entirely on the amount they sell, this direct result of your action, prompted by humane sentiment, will be to reduce still further these miserable earnings; that is to say, you increase the suffering of the very persons whose lot you desire to alleviate. You may say that you buy your matches all the same, but you buy them at a shop where you may or may not have reason to believe that the attendants are well paid. But that will not benefit the girls, whose business you have destroyed; they will not be employed in the shops, for they belong to a different grade of labour. This dilemma meets the social reformer at each step; the complexity of industrial relations appears to turn the chariot of progress into a Juggernaut's car, to crush a number of innocent victims with each advance it makes. One thing is evident, that if the consuming public were to regulate its acts of purchase with every possible regard to the condition of the workers, they could not ensure that every worker should have good regular work for decent wages.

In arriving at this conclusion, we are far from maintaining that the public even in its private capacity as a body of consumers could do nothing. A certain portion of responsibility rests on the public, as we saw it rested on employers and on middlemen. But the malady is rightly traceable in its full force neither to the action of individuals nor of industrial classes, but to the relation which subsists between these individuals and classes; that is, to the nature and character of the industrial system in its present working. This may seem a vague statement, but it is correct; the desire to be prematurely definite has led to a narrow conception of the "sweating" malady, which more than anything else has impeded efforts at reform.

CHAPTER V.

THE CAUSES OF SWEATING.

§ 1. The excessive Supply of Low-skilled Labour.—Turning to the industrial system for an explanation of the evils of "Sweating," we shall find three chief factors in the problem; three dominant aspects from which the question may be regarded. They are sometimes spoken of as the causes of sweating, but they are better described as conditions, and even as such are not separate, but closely related at various points.

The first condition of "sweating" is an abundant and excessive supply of low-skilled and inefficient labour. It needs no parade of economic reasoning to show that where there are more persons willing to do a particular kind of work than are required, the wages for that work, if free competition is permitted, cannot be more than what is just sufficient to induce the required number to accept the work. In other words, where there exists any quantity of unemployed competitors for low-skilled work, wages, hours of labour, and other conditions of employment are so regulated, as to present an attraction which just outweighs the alternatives open to the unemployed, viz. odd jobs, stealing, starving, and the poor-house. In countries where access to unused land is free, the productiveness of labour applied to such land marks the minimum of wages possible; in countries where no such access is possible, the minimum wages of unskilled labour, whenever the supply exceeds the demand, is determined by the attractiveness of the alternatives named above.

A margin of unemployed labour means a bare subsistence wage for low-skilled labour, and it means this wage earned under industrial conditions, such as we find under the "sweating system." In order to keep the wage of low-skilled labour down to this minimum, which can only rise with an improvement in the alternatives, it is not required that there should at any time exist a large number of unemployed. A very small number, in effective competition with those employed, will be quite as effectual in keeping down the rate of wages. The same applies to all grades of skilled labour, with this important difference, that the minimum wage can never fall below what is required to induce less skilled workers to acquire and apply the extra skill which will enable them to furnish the requisite supply of highly-skilled workers. Trade Unions have instinctively directed all their efforts to preventing the competition of unemployed workers in their respective trades from pulling down to its minimum the rate of wages. The strongest of those have succeeded in establishing a standard wage less than which no one shall accept; unemployed men, who in free competition would accept less than this standard wage, are supported by the funds of the Union, that they may not underbid. Unions of comparatively unskilled workers, who are never free from the competition of unemployed, and who cannot undertake permanently to buy off all competitors ready to underbid, endeavour to limit the numbers of their members, and to prevent outsiders from effectively competing with them in the labour market, in order that by restricting the supply of labour, they may prevent a fall of wages. The importance of these movements for us consists in their firm but tacit recognition of the fact, that an excessive supply of unskilled labour lies at the root of the industrial disease of "sweating."

§ 2. The Contributing Causes of excessive Supply.—The last two chapters have dealt with the principal large industrial movements which bear on this supply of excessive low-skilled labour; but to make the question clear, it will be well to enumerate the various contributing causes.

α. The influx of rural population into the towns constantly swells the supply of raw unskilled labour. The better quality of this agricultural labour, as we saw, does not continue to form part of this glut, but rises into more skilled and higher paid strata of labour. The worse quality forms a permanent addition to the mass of inefficient labour competing for bare subsistence wages.

β. The steady flow of cheap unskilled foreign labour into our large cities, especially into London, swollen by occasional floods of compulsory exiles, adds an element whose competition as a part of the mass of unskilled labour is injurious out of proportion to its numerical amount.

γ. Since this foreign immigration weakens the industrial condition of our low-skilled native labour by increasing the supply, it will be evident that any cause which decreases the demand for such labour will operate in the same way. The free importation from abroad of goods which compete in our markets with the goods which "sweated" labour is applied to make, has the same effect upon the workers in "sweating" trades as the introduction of cheap foreign labour. The one diminishes the demand, the other increases the supply of unskilled or low-skilled labour. The import of quantities of German-made cheap clothing into East London shops, to compete with native manufacture of the same goods, will have precisely the same force in maintaining "sweating," as will the introduction of German workers, who shall make these same clothes in East London itself. In each case, the purchasing public reaps the advantage of cheap labour in low prices, while the workers suffer in low wages. The contention that English goods made at home must be exported to pay for the cheap German goods, furnishes no answer from the point of view of the low-skilled worker, unless these exports embody the kind of labour of which he is capable.

δ. The constant introduction of new machinery, as a substitute for skilled hand-labour, by robbing of its value the skill of certain classes of workers, adds these to the supply of low-skilled labour.

ε. The growth of machinery and of education, by placing women and young persons more upon an equality with male adult labour, swells the supply of low-skilled labour in certain branches of work. Women and young persons either take the places once occupied by men, or undertake new work (e.g. in post-office or telegraph-office), which would once have been open only to the competition of men. This growth of the direct or indirect competition of women and young persons, must be considered as operating to swell the general supply of unskilled labour.

ζ. In London another temporary, but important, factor must be noted. The competition of provincial factories has proved too strong for London factories in many industries. Hence of late years a gradual transfer of manufacture from London to the provinces. A large number of workers in London factories have found themselves out of work. The break-up of the London factories has furnished "sweating trades" with a large quantity of unemployed and starving people from whom to draw.

Regarded from the widest economic point of view, the existence of an excessive supply of labour seeking employments open to free competition must be regarded as the most important aspect of the "sweating system." The recent condition of the competition for casual dock-labour brought dramatically to the foreground this factor in the labour question. The struggle for livelihood was there reduced to its lowest and most brutal terms. "There is a place at the London Docks called the cage, a sort of pen fenced off by iron railings. I have seen three hundred half-starved dockers crowded round this cage, when perhaps a ganger would appear wanting three hands, and the awful struggle of these three hundred famished wretches fighting for that opportunity to get two or three hours' work has left an impression upon me that can never be effaced. Why, I have actually seen them clambering over each other's backs to reach the coveted ticket. I have frequently seen men emerge bleeding and breathless, with their clothes pretty well torn off their backs." The competition described in this picture only differs from other competitions for low-skilled town labour in as much as the conditions of tender gave a tragical concentration to the display of industrial forces. This picture, exaggerated as it will appear to those who have not seen it, brings home to us the essential character of free competition for low-skilled labour where the normal supply is in excess of the demand. If other forms of low-skilled labour were put up to be scrambled for in the same public manner, the scene would be repeated *ad nauseam*. But because the competition of seamstresses, tailors, shirt-finishers, fur-sewers, &c., is conducted more quietly and privately, it is not less intense, not less miserable, and not less degrading. This struggle for life in the shape of work for bare subsistence wages, is the true logical and necessary outcome of free competition among an over supply of low-skilled labourers.

§ 3. The Multiplication of "Small Masters."—Having made so much progress in our analysis, we shall approach more intelligently another important aspect of the "sweating system." Mr. Booth and other investigators find the tap-root of the disease to consist in the multiplication of small masters. The leading industrial forces of the age, as we have seen, make for the concentration of labour in larger and larger masses, and its employment in larger and larger factories. Yet in London and in certain other large centres of population, we find certain trades which are still conducted on a small scale in little workshops or private houses, and those trades furnish a very large proportion of the worst examples of "sweating." Here is a case of arrested development in the evolution of industry. It is even worse than that; for some trades which had been subject to the concentrating force of the factory system, have fallen into a sort of back-wash of the industrial current, and broken up again into smaller units. The increased proportion of the clothing industries conducted in private houses and small workshops is the most notorious example. This applies not only to East London, but to Liverpool, Leeds, Sheffield, and other large cities, especially where foreign labour has penetrated. For a large proportion of the sweating workshops, especially in clothing trades, are supported by foreign labour. In Liverpool during the last ten years the substitution of home-workers for workers in tailors' shops has been marked, and

90

in particular does this growth of home-workers apply to women.

A credible witness before the Lords' Committee stated that "at the present moment it would be safe to say that two-thirds of the sweaters in Liverpool are foreigners," coming chiefly from Germany and Russian Poland. In Leeds sixteen years ago there were only twelve Jewish workshops; there are now some hundreds.

Since a very large proportion of the worst sweating occurs in trades where the work is given out, either directly or by the medium of sub-contract, to home-workers, it is natural that stress should be laid upon the small private workshops as the centre of the disease. If the work could only be got away from the home and the small workshop, where inspection is impracticable, and done in the factory or large workshop, where limitations of hours of labour and sanitary conditions could be enforced, where the force of public opinion could secure the payment of decent wages, and where organization among workers would be possible, the worst phases of the malady would disappear. The abolition of the small workshop is the great object of a large number of practical reformers who have studied the sweating system. The following opinion of an expert witness is endorsed by many students of the question—"If the employers were compelled to obtain workshops, and the goods were made under a factory system, we believe that they could be made quite as cheaply under that system, with greater comfort to the workers, in shorter hours; and that the profits would then be distributed among the workers, so that the public would obtain their goods at the same price."[25] It is maintained that the inferior qualities of shoes are produced and sold more cheaply in the United States by a larger use of machinery under the factory system, than in London under a sweating system, though wages are, of course, much higher in America. Moreover, many of the products of the London sweating trades are competing on almost equal terms with the products of provincial factories, where machines are used instead of hand-labour.

§ **4. Economic Advantages of "Small Workshops."**—The question we have to answer is this—Why has the small workshop survived and grown up in London and other large cities, in direct antagonism to the prevalent industrial movement of the age? It is evident that the small workshop system must possess some industrial advantages which enable it to hold its own. The following considerations throw light upon this subject.

1. A larger proportion of the work in sweating trades is work for which there is a very irregular demand. Irregularity of employment, or, more accurately speaking, insufficiency of employment—for the "irregularity" is itself regular—forms one of the most terrible phases of the sweating system. The lower you descend in the ranks of labour the worse it is. A large number of the trades, especially where women are employed, are trades where the elements of "season" and fashion enter in. But even those which, like tailoring, shirtmaking, shoemaking, furniture and upholstery, would seem less subject to periodic or purely capricious changes, are liable in fact to grave and frequent fluctuations of the market. The average employment in sweating trades is roughly estimated at three or four days in the week. There are two busy seasons lasting some six weeks each, when these miserable creatures are habitually overworked. "The remaining nine months," says Mr. Burnett, "do not average more than half time, especially among the lower grade workers."

This gives us one clue to the ability of the small workshop to survive—its superior flexibility from the point of view of the employer.

"High organization makes for regularity; low organization lends itself to the opposite. A large factory cannot stop at all without serious loss; a full-sized workshop will make great efforts to keep going; but the man who employs only two or three others in his own house can, if work fails, send them all adrift to pick up a living as best they can."[26]

Since a smaller sweating-master can set up business on some £2 capital, and does not expect to make much more profit as employer than as workman, he is able to change from one capacity to the other with great facility.

2. The high rent for large business premises, especially in London, makes for the small workshop or home-work system. The payment of rent is thus avoided by the business firm which is the real employer, and thrown upon the sub-contractor or the workers themselves, to be by them in their turn generally evaded by using the dwelling-room for a workshop. Thus one of the most glaring evils of the sweating system is seen to form a distinct economic advantage in the workshop, as compared with the large factory. The element of rent is practically eliminated as an industrial charge.

3. The evasion of the restrictions of the Factory Act must be regarded as another economic advantage. Excessive hours of labour when convenient, overcrowding in order to avoid rent, absence of proper sanitary conditions, are essential to the cheapest forms of production under present conditions. It does not pay either the employing firm or the sub-contractor to consider the health or even the life of the workers, provided that the state of the labour market is such that they can easily replace spent lives.

4. The inability to combine for their mutual protection and advantage of scattered employés working in small bodies, living apart, and unacquainted even with the existence of one another, is another "cheapness" of the workshop system.

5. The fact that so large a proportion of master-sweaters are Jews has a special significance. It seems to imply that the poorer class of immigrant Jews possess a natural aptitude for the position, and that their presence in our large cities furnishes the corner-stone of the vicious system. Independence and mastery are conditions which have a market value for all men, but especially for the timid and often down-trodden Jew. Most men will contentedly receive less as master than as servant, but especially the Jew. We saw that the immigrant Jew, by his capacities and inclinations, was induced to make special efforts

to substitute work of management for manual labour, and to become a profit-maker instead of a wage-earner. The Jew craves the position of a sweating-master, because that is the lowest step in a ladder which may lead to a life of magnificence, supported out of usury. The Jewish Board of Guardians in London, though its philanthropic action is on the whole more enlightened than that of most wealthy public bodies, has been responsible in no small measure for this artificial multiplication of small masters. A very large proportion of the funds which they dispensed was given or lent in small sums in order to enable poor Jews "to set up for themselves." The effect of this was twofold. It first assisted to draw to London numbers of continental Jews, who struggled as "greeners" under sweaters for six months, until they were qualified for assistance from the Jewish Board of Guardians. It then enabled them to set up as small masters, and sweat other "greeners" as they themselves were sweated. It was quite true that the object of such charity was the most useful which any society could undertake; namely, that of assisting the industrially weak to stand on their own legs. But it was unfortunately true that this early stage of independence was built upon the miserable dependence of other workers.

6. But while, as we see, there are many special conditions which, in London especially, favour the small workshop, the most important will be found to consist in the large supply of cheap unskilled labour. This is the real material out of which the small workshop system is built. In dealing with the other conditions, we shall find that they all presuppose this abundant supply of labour. If labour were more scarce, and wages therefore higher, the small workshop would be impossible, for the absolute economy of labour, effected by the factory organization with its larger use of machinery, would far outweigh the number of small economies which, as we have seen, at present in certain trades, favour and make possible the small workshop. Every limitation in the supply of this low-skilled labour, every expansion of the alternatives offered by emigration, access to free land, &c., will

be effectual in crushing a number of the sweating workshops, and favouring the large factory at their expense.

§ 5. Irresponsibility of Employers.—The third view of the sweating System lays stress upon its moral aspect, and finds its chief cause in the irresponsibility of the employer. Now we have already seen that this severance of the personal relation between employer and employed is a necessary result of the establishment of the large factory as the industrial unit, and of the ever-growing complexity of modern commerce. It is not merely that the widening gap of social position between employer and employed, and the increased number of the latter, make the previous close relation impossible. Quite as important is the fact that the real employer in modern industry is growing more "impersonal." What we mean is this. The nominal employer or manager is not the real employer. The real employer of labour is capital, and it is to the owners of the capital in any business that we must chiefly look for the exercise of such responsibility as rightly subsists between employer and employed. Now, while it is calculated that one-eighth of the business of England is in the hands of joint-stock companies, constituting far more than one-eighth of the large businesses, in the great majority of other cases, where business is conducted on a large scale, the head of the business is to a great extent a mere manager of other people's capital. Thus while the manager's sense of personal responsibility is weakened by the number of "hands" whom he employs, his freedom of action is likewise crippled by his obligation to subserve the interests of a body of capitalists who are in ignorance of the very names and number of the human beings whose destiny they are controlling. The severance of the real "employer" from his "hands" is thus far more complete than would appear from mere attention to the growth in the size of the average business. Now it must not be supposed that this severance of the personal relation between employer and employed is of necessity a loss to the latter. There is no reason to suppose that the close relation subsisting in the old days between the master and his journeymen and apprentices was as a rule idyllically beautiful. No doubt the control of the master was often vexatious and despotic. The tyranny of a heartless employer under the old system was probably much more injurious than the apathy of the most vulgar plutocrat of to-day. The employé under the modern system is less subject to petty spite and unjust interference on the part of his employer. In this sense he is more free. But on the other hand, he has lost that guarantee against utter destitution and degradation afforded by the humanity of the better class of masters. He has exchanged a human nexus for a "cash nexus." The nominal freedom of this cash relationship is in the case of the upper strata of workmen probably a real freedom; the irresponsibility of their employers has educated them to more self-reliance, and strengthened a healthy personality in them. It is the lower class of workers who suffer. More and more they need the humanity of the responsible employer to protect them against the rigours of the labour-market. The worst miseries of the early factory times were due directly to the break-up of the responsibility of employers. This was slowly recognized by the people of England, and the series of Factory Acts, Employers' Liability Acts, and other measures for the protection of labour, must be regarded as a national attempt to build up a compulsory legal responsibility to be imposed upon employers in place of a natural responsibility based on moral feeling. We draft legislation and appoint inspectors to teach employers their duty towards employés, and to ensure that they do it. Thus in certain industries we have patched up an artificial mechanism of responsibility.

Wherever this legal responsibility is not enforced in the case of low-skilled workers, we have, or are liable to have, "sweating." Glancing superficially at the small workshop or sweating-den, it might seem that this being a mere survival of the old system, the legal enforcement of responsibility would be unnecessary. But it is not a mere survival. In the small workshop of the old system the master was the real employer. In the modern "sweating" den he is not the real employer, but a mere link between the employing firm and the worker. From this point of view we must assign as the true cause of sweating, the evasion of the legal responsibility of the Factory Act rendered possible to firms which employ outside workers either directly or indirectly through the agency of "sweaters." Although it might be prudent as a means of breaking up the small workshop to attempt to impose upon the "middleman" the legal responsibility, genuine reform directed to this aspect of "sweating," can only operate by making the real employing firm directly responsible for the industrial condition of its outdoor direct or indirect employés.

This responsibility imposed by law has been strengthened as an effective safeguard of the interests of the workers by combination among the latter. In skilled industries where strong trade organization exists, the practical value of such combination exceeds the value of restrictive legislation.

"In their essence Trade Unions are voluntary associations of workmen, for mutual protection and assistance in securing the most favourable conditions of labour." "This is their primary and fundamental object, and includes all efforts to raise wages or prevent a reduction of wages; to diminish the hours of labour or resist attempts to increase the working hours; and to regulate all matters pertaining to methods of employment or discharge, and modes of working."[27] Engineers, boiler-makers, cotton-spinners, printers, would more readily give up the assistance given them by legislative restriction than the power which they have secured for themselves by combination. It is in proportion as trade combination is weak that the actual protection afforded by Factory and Employers' Liability Acts become important. Just as we saw that sweating trades were those which escaped the legislative eye; so we see that they are also the trades where effective combination does not exist. Where Trade Unions are strong, sweating cannot make any way. The State aid of restrictive legislation, and the self help of private combination are alike wanting to the "sweated" workers.

CHAPTER VI.

_____

REMEDIES FOR SWEATING.

§ 1. Factory Legislation. What it can do.—Having now set forth the three aspects of the industrial disease of "Sweating"— the excessive supply of unskilled labour, the multiplication of small employers, the irresponsibility of capital—we have next to ask, What is the nature of the proposed remedies? Since any full discussion of the different remedies is here impossible, it must suffice if we briefly indicate the application of the chief proposed remedies to the different aspects of the disease. These remedies will fairly fall into three classes.

The first class aim at attacking by legislative means, the small workshop system, and the evils of long hours and unsanitary conditions from which the "sweated" workers suffer. Briefly, it may be said that they seek to increase and to enforce the legal responsibility of employers, and indirectly to crush the small workshop system by turning upon it the wholesome light of publicity, and imposing certain irksome and expensive conditions which will make its survival in its worst and ugliest shapes impossible. The most practical recommendation of the Report of the Lords' Committee is an extension of the sanitary clauses of the Factory Act, so as to reach all workshops.

We have seen that the unrestricted use of cheap labour is the essence of "sweating." If the wholesome restrictions of our Factory Legislation were in fact extended so as to cover all forms of employment, they would so increase the expenses of the sweating houses, that they would fall before the competition of the large factory system. Karl Marx writing a generation ago saw this most clearly. "But as regards labour in the so-called domestic industries, and the intermediate forms between this and manufacture, so soon as limits are put to the working day and to the employment of children, these industries go to the wall. Unlimited exploitation of cheap labour power is the sole foundation of their power to compete."[28]

The effectiveness of the existing Factory Act, so far as relates to small workshops, is impaired by the following considerations—

1. The difficulty in finding small workshops. There is no effectual registration of workshops, and the number of inspectors is inadequate to the elaborate and tedious method of search imposed by the present system.

2. The limitation as to right of entry. The power of inspectors to "enter, inspect, and examine at all reasonable times by day or night, a factory or a workshop, and every part thereof, when he has reason to believe that any person is employed therein, and to enter by day any place he has reasonable cause to believe to be a factory or workshop," is in fact not applicable in the case of dwelling-rooms used for workshops. In a large number of cases of the worst form of "sweating," the inspector has no right of entrance but by consent of the occupant, and the time which elapses before such consent is given suffices to enable the "sweater" to adjust matters so as to remove all evidence of infringements of the law.

3. The restricted power in reference to sanitation. A factory inspector has no sanitary powers; he cannot act save through the sanitary officer. The machinery of sanitary reform thus loses effectiveness.

Compulsory registration of workshops, adequate inspection, and reform of machinery of sanitary reform, would be of material value in dealing with some of the evils of the small workshop. But it would by no means put an end to "sweating." So far as it admitted the continuance of the small workshop, it would neither directly nor indirectly abate the evil of low wages. It is even possible that any rapid extension of the Factory Act might, by limiting the amount of employment in small workshops, increase for a time the misery of those low-skilled workers, who might be incapable of undertaking regular work in the larger factory. It is, at any rate, not evident that such legislative reform would assist low-class workers to obtain decent wages and regular employment, though it would improve the other conditions under which they worked.

Again, existing factory legislation by no means covers even theoretically the whole field of "sweating." Public-houses, restaurants, all shops and places of amusement, laundries, and certain other important forms of employment, which escape the present factory legislation, are in their lower branches liable to the evils of "sweating," and should be included under such factory legislation as seeks to remedy these evils.

§ 2. Co-operative Production.—The organization of labour is the second form of remedy. It is urged that wherever effective organization exists in any trade, there is no danger of sweating. We have therefore, it is maintained, only to organize the lower grades of labour, and "sweating" will cease to exist. There are two forms of organization commonly advocated, Co-operation and Trade Unionism.

The suggestion that the poorer grades of workers should by co-operative production seek to relieve themselves from the stress of poverty and the tyranny of the "sweating system," is a counsel of perfection far removed from the possibility of present attainment. No one who has closely studied the growth of productive co-operation in England will regard it as a practicable remedy for poverty. Productive co-operation is successful at present only in rare cases among skilled workmen of exceptional morale and education. It is impossible that it should be practised by low-skilled, low-waged workers, under industrial conditions like those of to-day. It is surprising to find that the Lords' Committee in its final report should have given prominence to schemes of co-operation as a cure for the disease. The following paragraph correctly sums up experience upon the subject—

"Productive societies have been from time to time started in East London, but their career has been neither long nor brilliant. They have often had a semi-philanthropic basis, and have been well-meant but hopeless attempts to supersede "sweating" by co-operation. None now working are of sufficient importance to be mentioned."[29]

The place which productive and distributive co-operation is destined to occupy in the history of the industrial freedom and elevation of the masses doubtless will be of the first importance. To look forward to a time when the workers of the community may be grouped in co-operative bodies, either competing with one another, or related by some bond which shall minimize the friction of competition, while not impairing the freedom and integrity of each several group, is not perhaps a wild utopian vision. To students of English industrial history the transition to such a state will not appear more marked than the transition through which industry passed under the Industrial Revolution to the present capitalist system. But the recognition of this possible future does not justify us in suggesting productive co-operation as a present remedy for the poverty of low-skilled city workers. These latter must rise several steps on the industrial and moral ladder before they are brought within the reach of the co-operative remedy. It is with the cost and labour of these early steps that the students of the problem of present poverty must concern themselves.

§ 3. Trade Unionism. Ability of Workers to combine. Trade Unionism is a more hopeful remedy. Large bodies of workers have by this means helped to raise themselves from a condition of industrial weakness to one of industrial strength. Why should not close combination among workers in low-paid and sweating industries be attended with like results? Why should not the men and women working in "sweating" trades combine, and insist upon higher wages, shorter hours, more regular employment, and better sanitary conditions? Well, it may be regarded as an axiom in practical economies, that any concerted action, however weak and desultory, has its value. Union is always strength. An employer who can easily resist any number of individual claims for higher wages by his power to replace each worker by an outsider, can less easily resist the united pressure of a large body of his workmen, because the inconvenience of replacing them all at once by a body of outsiders, is far greater than the added difficulty of replacing each of them at separate intervals of time. This is the basis of the power of concerted action among workers. But the measure of this power depends in the main upon two considerations.

First comes the degree of effectiveness in combination. The prime requisites for effective combination are a spirit of comradeship and mutual trust, knowledge and self-restraint in the disposition of united force. Education and free and frequent intercourse can alone establish these elements of effective combination. And here the first difficulty for workers in "sweating" trades appears. Low-skilled work implies a low degree of intelligence and education. The sweating industries, as we have seen, are as a rule those which escape the centralizing influence of the factory System, and where the employés work, either singly or in small groups, unknown to one another, and with few opportunities of forming a close mutual understanding. In some employments this local severance belongs to the essence of the work, as, for example, in the case of cab-drivers, omnibus-drivers, and generally in shop-work, where, in spite of the growth of large stores, small masters still predominate; in other employments the disunion of workers forms a distinct commercial advantage which enables such low-class industries to survive, as in the small workshop and the home-labour, which form the central crux of our sweating problem. The very lack of leisure, and the incessant strain upon the physique which belong to "sweating," contribute to retard education, and to render mutual acquaintanceship and the formation of a distinct trade interest extremely difficult. How to overcome these grave difficulties which stand in the way of effective combination among unskilled workers is a consideration of the first importance. The rapid and momentarily successful action of organized dock labourers must not be taken as conclusive evidence that combination in all other branches of low-class labour can proceed at the same pace. The public and localized character of the competition for casual dock labour rendered effective combination here possible, in spite of the low intellectual and moral calibre of the average labourer. It is the absence of such public and localized competition which is the kernel of the difficulty in most "sweating" trades. It may be safely said that the measure of progress in organization of low class labour will be the comparative size and localization of the industrial unit. Where "sweating" exists in large factories or large shops, effective combination even among workers of low education may be tolerably rapid; among workers engaged by some large firm whose work brings them only into occasional contact, the progress will be not so fast; among workers in small unrelated workshops who have no opportunities of direct intercourse with one another, the progress will be extremely slow. The most urgent need of organization is precisely in those industries where it is most difficult to organize. It is, on the whole, not reasonable to expect that this remedy, unless aided by other forces working against the small workshops, will enable the "hands" in the small sweater's den to materially improve their condition.

§ 4. **Trade Union Methods of limiting Competition.**—So far we have regarded the value of combination as dependent on the ability of workers to combine. There is another side which cannot be neglected. Two societies of workmen equally strong in the moral qualities of successful union may differ widely in the influence they can exert to secure and improve their position. We saw that the real value of organization to a body of workmen lay in the power it gave them to make it inconvenient for an employer to dispense with their services in favour of outsiders. Now the degree of this inconvenience will obviously depend in great measure upon the number of outsiders qualified by strength and skill to take their place without delay. The whole force of Unionism hangs on "the unemployed." The strongest and most effective Unions are in trades where there are the smallest number of unemployed competitors; the weakest Unions are in trades which are beset by crowds of outsiders able and willing to undertake the work, and if necessary to underbid those who are employed.

Close attention to the composition and working of our Trade Unions discloses the fact that their chief object is to limit the competition for work in their respective trades. Since their methods are sometimes indirect, this is sometimes denied, but the following statement of Trade Union methods makes it clear. The minimum or standard rate of wages plays a prominent part in Unionism. It is arbitrarily fixed by the Union, which in its estimate takes into account, α. prices paid for articles produced; β. a reasonable standard of comfort; γ. and remuneration for time spent in acquiring necessary skill.[30] This is an estimate, it must be remembered, of a "fair wage," based upon calculations as to what is just and reasonable, and does not necessarily correspond to the economic wage obtainable in a neighbourhood by the free competition of labour and capital. Now this standard wage, which may or may not be the wage actually paid, plays a very prominent part in Unionism. The point of importance here is its bearing on the admission of new members. The candidate for membership has, as his principal qualification, to show that he is capable of earning the standard rate of wages. It is evident, however, that the effect of any large new accession to the ranks of any trade must, unless there is a corresponding growth of employment, bring down the rate of wages, whether these be fixed by a Trade Union standard or not. Hence it is evident that any Trade Union would be bound to refuse admission to new applicants who, though they might be in other respects competent workmen, could not find work without under-bidding those who were at present occupied. This they would do by reason of their standard wage qualification, for they would be able to show that the new applicants would not be competent to earn standard wages under the circumstances. How far Trade Unions actually have conscious recourse to this method of limiting their numbers, may be doubted; but no one acquainted with the spirit of Trades Unions would believe that if a sudden growth of technical schools enabled large numbers of duly qualified youths to apply for admission into the various Unions so as to compete for the same quantity of work with the body of existing members, the Unions of the latter would freely and cheerfully admit them. To do so would be suicidal, for no standard rate of wages could stand against the pressure of an increased supply of labour upon a fixed demand. But it is not necessary to suppose that any considerable number of actually qualified workmen are refused admission to Trade Unions of skilled workers. For the possession of the requisite skill, implying as it does a certain natural capacity, and an expenditure of time and money not within the power of the poorest classes, forms a practical limit to the number of applicants. Moreover, in many trades, though by no means in all, restrictions are placed by the Unions upon the number of apprentices, with the object of limiting the number of those who should from year to year be qualified to compete for work. In other trades where no rigid rule to this effect exists, there is an understanding which is equally effective. Certain trades, such as the engineers, boiler-makers, and other branches of iron trade, place no restrictions, and in certain other trades the restrictions are not closely applied. But most of the strong Trades Unions protect themselves in another way against the competition of unemployed. By a System of "out of work" pay, they bribe those of their body, who from time to time are thrown out of work, not to underbid those in work, so as to bring down the rate of wages. Several of the most important Unions pay large sums every year to "out of work" members. By these three means, the "minimum wage" qualification for membership, the limitation of the number of apprentices, and the "out of work" fund, the Trade Unions strengthen the power of organized labour in skilled industries by restricting the competition of unemployed outsiders.

It is true that some of the leading exponents of Trade Unionism deny that the chief object of the Unions is to limit competition. Mr. Howell considers that the "standard wage" qualification for membership is designed in order to ensure a high standard of workmanship, and regards the "out of work" fund merely as belonging to the insurance or prudential side of Trade Unionism. But though it may readily be admitted that one effect of these measures may be to maintain good workmanship and to relieve distress, it is reasonable to regard the most important result actually attained as being the object chiefly sought. It is fair to suppose, therefore, that while Unionists may not be indifferent to the honour of their craft, their principal object is to strengthen their economic position. At any rate, whatever the intention of Trade Unions may be, the principal effect of their regulations is to limit the effective supply of competing labour in their respective branches of industry.

§ 5. Can Low-skilled Workers successfully combine?—Now the question which concerns our inquiry may be stated thus. Supposing that the workers in "sweating" industries were able to combine, would they be able to secure themselves against outside competition as the skilled worker does? Will their combination practically increase the difficulty in replacing them by outsiders? Now it will be evident that the unskilled or low-skilled workers cannot depend upon the methods which are adopted by Unions of skilled workers, to limit the number of competitors for work. A test of physical fitness, such as was recently proposed as a qualification for admission to the Dock-labourers Union, will not, unless raised far above the average fitness of present members, limit the number of applicants to anything like the same extent as the test of workmanship in skilled industries. Neither could rules of apprenticeship act where the special skill required was very small. Nor again is it easy to see how funds raised by the contribution of the poorest classes of workers, could suffice to support unemployed members when temporarily "out of work," or to buy off the active competition of outsiders, or "black-legs," to use the term in vogue. The constant influx of unskilled labour from the rural districts and from abroad, swollen by the numbers of skilled workmen whose skill has been robbed of its value by machinery, keeps a large continual margin of unemployed, able and willing to undertake any kind of unskilled or low-skilled labour, which will provide a minimum subsistence wage. The very success which attends the efforts of skilled workers to limit the effective supply of their labour by making it more difficult for unskilled workers to enter their ranks, increases the competition for low-skilled work, and makes effective combination among low-skilled workers more difficult. Though we may not be inclined to agree with Prof. Jevons, that "it is quite impossible for Trade Unions in general to effect any permanent increase of wages," there is much force in his conclusion, that "every rise of wages which one body secures by mere exclusive combination, represents a certain extent, sometimes a large extent, of injury to the other bodies of workmen."[31] In so far as Unions of skilled workers limit their numbers, they increase the number of competitors for unskilled work; and since wages cannot rise when the supply of labour obtainable at the present rate exceeds the demand, their action helps to maintain that "bare subsistence wage," which forms a leading feature in "sweating."

Are we then to regard Unions of low-skilled workers as quite impotent so long as they are beset by the competition of innumerable outsiders? Can combination contribute nothing to a solution of the sweating problem? There are two ways in which close combination might seem to avail low-skilled workers in their endeavours to secure better industrial conditions.

In the first place, close united action of a large body of men engaged in any employment gives them, as we saw, a certain power dependent on the inconvenience and expense they can cause to their employers by a sudden withdrawal. This power is, of course, in part measured by the number of unemployed easily procurable to take their place. But granted the largest possible margin of unemployed, there will always be a certain difficulty and loss in replacing a united body of employés by a body of outsiders, though the working capacity of each new-comer may be equal to that of each member of the former gang. This power belonging inherently to those in possession, and largely dependent for its practical utility on close unity of action, may always be worked by a trade organization to push the interests of its members independently of the supply of free outside labour, and used by slow degrees may be made a means of gaining piece by piece a considerable industrial gain. Care must, however, be taken, never to press for a larger gain than is covered by the difficulty of replacing the body of present employés by outside labour. Miscalculations of the amount of this inherent power of Union are the chief causes of "lock-outs" and failures in strikes.

Another weapon in the hands of unskilled combination, less calculable in its effectiveness, is the force of public opinion aided by "picketing," and the other machinery of persuasion or coercion used to prevent the effective competition of "free" labour. In certain crises, as for example in the Dock strike of 1889, these forces may operate so powerfully as to strictly limit the supply of labour, and to shut out the competition of unemployed. There can be no reason to doubt that if public authority had not winked at illegal coercion of outside labour, and public opinion touched by sentiment condoned the winking, the Dock strike would have failed as other movements of low-skilled labour have generally failed. The success of the Dockers is no measure of the power of combination among low-skilled labourers. It is possible, however, that a growing sense of comradeship, aided by a general recognition of the justice of a claim, may be generally relied upon to furnish a certain force which shall restrict the competition of free labour in critical junctures of the labour movement. If public opinion, especially among workmen, becomes strongly set in favour of letting capital and labour "fight it out" in cases of trade disputes, and vigorously resents all interference of outsiders offering to replace the contending labourers, it seems likely that this practical elimination of outside competition may enable combinations of unskilled workmen to materially improve their condition in spite of the existence of a large supply of outside labour able to replace them.

§ 6. **Can Trade Unionism crush out "Sweating"?**—But here again it must be recognized that each movement of public opinion in this direction is really making for the establishment of new trade monopolies, which tend to aggravate the condition of free unemployed labour. Unions of low-skilled labour can only be successful at the expanse of outsiders, who will find it increasingly difficult to get employment. The success of combinations of low-skilled workers will close one by one every avenue of regular employment to the unemployed, who will tend to become even more nomadic and predatory in their habits, and more irregular and miserable in their lives, affording continually a larger field of operation for the small "sweater," and other forms of "arrested development" in commerce. It must always be an absorbing interest to a Trades Union to maintain the industrial welfare of its members by preventing what it must regard as an "over-supply" of labour. No organization of labour can effect very much unless it takes measures to restrict the competition of "free labour"; each Union, by limiting the number of competitors for its work, increases the competition in trades not similarly protected. So with every growth of Trade Unionism the pressure on unprotected bodies of workmen grows greater. Thus it would seem that while organization of labour may become a real remedy for "sweating" in any industry to which it is vigorously applied, it cannot be relied upon ever entirely to crash out the evil. It can only drive it into a smaller compass, where its intenser character may secure for it that close and vigorous public attention which, in spite of recent revelations, has not been yet secured, and compel society to clearly face the problem of a residue of labour-power which is rotting in the miserable and degraded bodies of its owners, because all the material on which it might be productively employed is otherwise engaged.

§ 7. **Public Workshops.**—Those who are most active in the spread of Unionism among the low-skilled branches of industry, are quite aware that their action, by fencing off section after section of labour from the fierce competition of outsiders, is rendering the struggle more intense for the unprotected residuum. So far as they indulge any wider view than the interest of their special trades, it may be taken that they design to force the public to provide in some way for the unemployed or casually employed workers, against whom the gates of each Union have been successively closed. There can be little doubt that if Unionism is able to establish itself firmly among the low-skilled industries, we shall find this margin of unemployed low-skilled labour growing larger and more desperate, in proportion to the growing difficulty of finding occupation. Trade Union leaders have boldly avowed that they will thus compel the State to recognize the "right to employment," and to provide that employment by means of national or municipal workshops. With questions of abstract "right" we are not here concerned, but it may be well to indicate certain economic difficulties involved in the establishment of public works as a solution of the "unemployed" problem. Since the "unemployed" will, under the closer restrictions of growing Trade Unionism, consist more and more of low-skilled labourers, the public works on which they must be employed must be branches of low-skilled labour. But the Unions of low-skilled workers will have been organized with the view of monopolizing all the low-skilled work which the present needs of the community require to be done. How then will the public provide low-skilled work for the unemployed? One of two courses seems inevitable. Either the public must employ them in work similar to that which is being done by Union men for private firms, in which case they will enter into competition with the latter, and either undersell them in the market and take their trade, or by increasing the aggregate supply of the produce, bring down the price, and with it the wage of the Union men. Or else if they are not to compete with the labour of Union men,

110

they must be employed in relief works, undertaken not to satisfy a public need or to produce a commodity with a market value, but in order that those employed may, by a wholly or partially idle expenditure of effort, appear to be contributing to their own support, whereas they are really just as much recipients of public charity as if they were kept in actual idleness. This is the dilemma which has to be faced by advocates of public workshops. Nor can it be eluded by supposing that the public may use the unemployed labour either in producing some new utility for the public use, such as improved street-paving, or a municipal hot-water supply. For if such undertakings are of a character which a private company would regard as commercially sound, they ought to be, and will be, undertaken by wise public bodies independently of the consideration of providing work for unemployed. If they are not such as would be considered commercially sound, then in so far as they fall short of commercial soundness, they will be "charity" pure and simple, given as relief is now given to able-bodied paupers, on condition of an expenditure of mere effort which is not a commercial *quid pro quo*.

If the State or municipality were permitted to conduct business on ordinary commercial principles, it might indeed be expected to seize the opportunity afforded by a large supply of unemployed labour, to undertake new public works at a lower cost than usual. But to take this advantage of the cheapness of labour is held to be "sweating." Public bodies are called upon to disregard the rise and fall of market wages, and to pay "a fair wage," which practically means a wage which is the same whether labour is plentiful or scarce. This refusal to permit the ordinary commercial inducement to operate in the case of public bodies, cuts off what might be regarded as a natural check to the accumulation of unemployed labour. If public bodies are to employ more labour, when labour is excessive, and pay a wage which shall be above the market price, it must be clearly understood that the portion of the wages which represents the "uncommercial" aspect of the contract is just as much public charity as the half-crown paid as out-door relief under the present Poor Law. Lastly, the establishment of State or municipal workshops for the "unemployed" has no economic connection with the "socialist" policy, by which the State or municipality should assume control and management of railways, mines, gas-works, tramways, and other works into which the element of monopoly enters. Such a "socialist" policy, if carried out, would not directly afford any relief to the unemployed. For, in the first place, the labour employed in these new public departments would be chiefly skilled, and not unskilled. Moreover, so far as the condition of the "workers" was concerned, the nationalization, or municipalization of these works would not imply any increased demand for labour, but merely the transfer of a number of employés from private to the public service. The public control of departments of industry, which are now in private hands, would not, so long as it was conducted on a commercial footing in the public interest, furnish either direct, or indirect, relief to "the unemployed." A reduction of hours of labour in the case of workers transferred to the public service, might afford employment to an increased number of skilled labourers, and might indirectly operate in reducing the number of unemployed. But such reduction of hours of labour, like the payment of wages above the market rate, forms no essential part of a "socialist" policy, but is rather a charitable appendage.

§ 8. **State Business on uncommercial terms.**—It cannot be too clearly recognized that the payment by a public body of wages which are above the market price, the payment of pensions, the reduction of hours of labour, and any other advantages freely conferred, which place public servants in a better position than private servants, stand on precisely the same economic footing with the establishment of public workshops for the relief of the unemployed, in which wages are paid for work which is deficient in commercial value. In each case the work done has some value, unless the unemployed are used to dig holes in the ground and fill them up again; in each case the wages paid for that work are in excess of the market rate.

If it were established as a general rule, that public bodies should always add a "bonus" to the market wage of their employés to bring it up to "fairness," and take off a portion of the usual "working-day" to bring it down to "fairness," it would follow quite consistently that a wage equal to, or exceeding, the minimum market rate might be paid to "unemployed" for work, the value of which would be somewhat less than that produced by the lowest class of "employed" workers. The policy throughout is one and the same, and is based upon a repudiation of competition as a test of the value of labour, and the substitution of some other standard derived from moral or prudential considerations.

So far as the State or Municipality chooses to regulate by an "uncommercial" or moral standard the conditions of labour for the limited number of employés required for the services which are a public monopoly, it is able to do so, provided the public is willing to pay the price. There is much to be said in favour of such a course, for the public example might lend invaluable aid in forming a strong public opinion which should successfully demand decent conditions of life and work, for the whole body of workers. But if the State or Municipality were to undertake to provide work and wages for an indefinite number of men who failed to obtain work in the competition market, the effect would be to offer a premium upon "unemployment." Thus, it would appear that as fast as the public works drew off the unemployed, so fast would men leave the low-paid, irregular occupations, and by placing themselves in a state of "unemployment" qualify for public service. There would of course be a natural check to this flow. As the State drained off all surplus labour, the market value of labour would rise, greater regularity of employment would be secured, and the general improvement of industrial conditions would check the tendency of workers to flow towards the public workshops. This consideration has led many of the leaders of labour movements to favour a scheme of public workshops, which would practically mean that the State or Municipality undertook to limit the supply of labour in the open market, by providing for any surplus which might exist, at the public expense. The effect of such a policy would be of course to enormously strengthen the effective power of labour-organizations. But while the advocates of public workshops are fully alive to these economic effects, they have not worked out with equal clearness the question relating to the disposal of the labour in public workshops. How can the "protected" labour of the public workshops be so occupied, that its produce may not, by direct or indirect competition with the produce of outside labour, outweigh the advantage conferred upon the latter by the removal of the "unemployed" from the field of competition, in digging holes and filling them up again, or other useless work, the problem is a simple one. In that case the State provides maintenance for the weaker members in order that their presence as competitors for work may not injure the stronger members. But if the public workmen produce anything of value, by what means can it be kept from competing with and underselling the goods produced under ordinary commercial conditions? Without alleging that the difficulties involved in these questions are necessarily fatal to all schemes of public works, we maintain that they require to be clearly faced.

Even if it be held that public workshops can furnish no economic remedy for poverty, this judgment would of course be by no means conclusive against public emergency works undertaken on charitable grounds to tide over a crisis. Every form of charity, public or private, discriminate or indiscriminate, entails some evil consequences. But this consideration is not final. A charitable palliative is defensible and useful when the net advantages outweigh the net disadvantages. This might seem self-evident, but it requires to be stated, because there are not wanting individuals and societies which imagine they have disposed of the claim of charitable remedies by pointing out the evil consequences they entail. It is evident that circumstances might arise which would compel the wisest and steadiest Government to adopt public relief works as a temporary expedient for meeting exceptional distress.

§ 9. **Restriction of Foreign Emigration.**—Two further proposals for keeping down the supply of low-skilled labour deserve notice, and the more so because they are forcing their way rapidly toward the arena of practical politics.

The first is the question of an Alien law limiting or prohibiting the migration of foreign labourers into England. The power of the German, Polish, or Russian Jew, accustomed to a lower standard of life, to undersell the English worker in the English labour market, has already been admitted as a cause of "sweating" in several city industries. The importance of this factor in the problem of poverty is, however, a much disputed point. To some extent these foreign labourers are said to make new industries, and not to enter into direct and disastrous competition with native workers. In most cases, however, direct competition between foreign and native workers does exist, and, as we see, the comparatively small number of the foreign immigrants compared with the aggregate of native workers, is no true criterion of the harm their competition does to low-waged workers. Whether this country will find it wise to reverse its national policy of free admission to outside labour, it is not easy to predict. The point should not be misunderstood. Free admission of cheap foreign labour must be admitted *primâ facie* to be conducive to the greatest production of wealth in this country. Those who seek to restrict or prohibit this admission, do so on the ground that the damage inflicted upon that class of workers, brought directly or indirectly into competition for employment with these foreigners, overbalances the net gain in the aggregate of national wealth. It is this consideration which has chiefly operated in inducing the United States, Canada, and Australia to prohibit the admission of Chinese or Coolie labour, and to place close restrictions upon cheap European labour. Sir Charles Dilke, in a general summary of colonial policy on this matter, writes, "Colonial labour seeks protection by legislative means, not only against the cheap labour of the dark-skinned or of the yellow man, but also against white paupers, and against the artificial supply of labour by State-aided white immigration. Most of the countries of the world, indeed, have laws against the admission of destitute aliens, and the United Kingdom is in practice almost the only exception."[32]

The greater contrast between the customary standard of living of the immigrants and that of the native workers with whom they would compete, has naturally made the question seem a more vital one for our colonies, and for the United States than for us. There can, however, be little doubt that if a few shiploads of Chinese labourers were emptied into the wharves of East London, whatever Government chanced to be in power would be compelled to adopt immediate measures of restraint on immigration, so terrible would the effect be upon the low class European labourers in our midst. Whether any such Alien legislation will be adopted to meet the inroad of continental labour depends in large measure on the course of continental history. It is, however, not improbable that if the organization of the workers proceeds along the present lines, when they come to realize their ability to use political power for securing their industrial position, they may decide that it will be advisable to limit the supply of labour by excluding foreigners. Those, however, who are already prepared to adopt such a step, do not always realize as clearly as they should, that the exclusion of cheap foreigners from our labour-market will be in all probability accompanied by an exclusion from our markets of the cheap goods made by these foreigners in their own country, the admission of which, while it increases the aggregate wealth of England, inflicts a direct injury on those particular workers, the demand for whose labour is diminished by the introduction of foreign goods which can undersell them. If an Alien law is passed, it will bring both logically and historically in its wake such protective measures as will constitute a reversal of our present Free Trade policy. Whether such new and hazardous changes in our national policy are likely to be made, depends

116

in large measure upon the success of other schemes for treating the condition of over-supply of low-skilled labour. If no relief is found from these, it seems not unlikely that a democratic government will some day decide that such artificial prohibition of foreign labour, and the foreign goods which compete with the goods produced by low-skilled English labour, will benefit the low-skilled workers in their capacity as wage-earners, more than the consequent rise of prices will injure them in their capacity as consumers.

§ 10. The "Eight Hours Day" Argument.—The last proposal which deserves attention, is that which seeks to shorten the average working-day. The attempt to secure by legislation or by combination an eight hours day, or its equivalent, might seem to affect the "sweating system" most directly, as a restriction on excessive hours of labour. But so far as it claims to strike a blow at the industrial oppression of low-skilled labour, its importance will depend upon its effect on the demand and supply of that low-skilled labour. The result which the advocates of an eight hours day claim for their measure, may be stated as follows—

Assuming that low-skilled workers now work on an average twelve hours a day, a compulsory reduction to eight hours would mean that one-third more men were required to perform the same amount of work, leaving out for convenience the question whether an eight hours day would be more productive than the first eight hours of a twelve hours day. Since the same quantity of low-skilled work would require to be done, employment would now be provided for a large number of those who would otherwise have been unemployed. In fact, if the shorter day is accompanied by an absolute prohibition of over-time, it seems possible that work would thus be found for the whole army of "unemployed." Nor is this all. The existence of a constant standing "pool" of unemployed was, as we saw, responsible for keeping the wages of low-skilled labour down to a bare subsistence wage. Let this "pool" be once drained off, wages will rapidly rise, since the combined action of workers will no longer be able to be defeated by the eagerness of "outsiders" to take their work and wages. Thus an eight hours day would at once solve the problem of the "work-less," and raise the wages of low-skilled labour. The effect would be precisely the same as if the number of competitors for work were suddenly reduced. For the price of labour, as of all else, depends on the relation between the demand for it and the supply, and the price will rise if the demand is increased while the supply remains the same, or if the supply is decreased while the demand remains the same. A compulsory eight hours day would practically mean a shrinkage in the supply of labour offered in the market, and the first effect would indisputably be a rise in the price of labour. To reduce by one-third at a single blow the amount of labour put forth in a day by any class of workers, is precisely equivalent to a sudden removal of one-third of these workers from the field of labour. We know from history that the result of a disastrous epidemic, like the Black Plague, has been to raise the wages and improve the general condition of the labourer even in the teeth of legal attempts to keep down wages. The advocates of an Eight Hours Act assert that the same effect would follow from that measure.

Setting aside as foreign to our discussion all consideration of the difficulties in passing and enforcing an Eight Hours Act, or in applying it to certain industries, the following economic objection is raised by opponents to the eight hours movement—

The larger aggregate of wages, which must be paid under an eight hours day, will increase the expanses of production in each industry. For the increased wage cannot in general be obtained by reducing profits, for any such reduction will drive freshly-accumulated capital more and more to seek foreign investments, and managing ability will in some measure tend to follow it. The higher aggregate of wages must therefore be represented in a general rise of prices. This rise of prices will have two effects. In the first place it will tend to largely negative the higher aggregate of money wages. Or if organized labour, free from the competition of unemployed, is able to maintain a higher rate of real wages, the general rise in prices will enable foreign producers to undersell us in our own market (unless we adopted a Protective Tariff), and will disable us from competing in foreign markets. This constitutes the pith of the economic objection raised against an eight hours day. The eight hours advocates meet the objection in the following ways—First, they deny that prices will rise in consequence of the increased aggregate of wages. A reduction in interest and in wages of superintendence will take place in many branches of industry, without any appreciable tendency to diminish the application of capital, or to drive it out of the country.

Secondly, the result of an increased expenditure in wages will be to crush the small factories and workshops, which are the backbone of the sweating System, and to assist the industrial evolution which makes in favour of large well-organized factories working with the newest machinery.

Thirdly, it is claimed that we shall not be ousted either from our own or from foreign markets by foreign competition, because the eight hours movement in England must be regarded as part of a larger industrial movement which is proceeding *pari passu* among the competing nations. If the wages of German, French, and American workers are advancing at the same rate as English wages, or if other industrial restrictions in those countries are otherwise increasing the expenses of production at a corresponding rate, the argument of foreign competition falls to the ground.

These leading arguments of the advocates of an eight hours day are of very unequal value. The first argument is really based upon the supposition that the increased aggregate of wages can be "got out of capital" by lowering interest and profits. The general validity of this argument may be questioned. In its application a distinction must be drawn between those businesses which by means of the possession of some monopoly, patent, or other trade advantage are screened from the full force of competition, and are thus enabled to earn profits above the average, and those businesses where the constant stress of close competition keeps interest and profits down to the lowest point which suffices to induce the continued application of capital and organizing ability. In the former cases the "cost" of an Eight Hours Day might be got out of capital, assuming an effective organization of labour, in the latter cases it could not.

As to the second argument, it is probable enough that the legal eight hours day would accelerate the industrial evolution, which is enabling the large well-equipped factory to crush out the smaller factory. As we have seen that the worst evils of "sweating" are associated with a lower order of industrial organization, any cause which assisted to destroy the small workshop and the out-work system, would be a benefit. But as the economic motive of such improved organization with increased use of machinery, would be to save human labour, it is doubtful whether a quickening of this process would not act as a continual feeder to the band of unemployed, by enabling employers to dispense with the services of even this or that body of workers whose work is taken over by brute machinery.

The net value of these two eight hours arguments is doubtful. The real weight of the discussion seems to rest on the third.

If the movement for improving the industrial condition of the working classes does proceed as rapidly in other industrial countries as in our own, we shall have nothing to fear from foreign competition, since expenses of production and prices will be rising equally among our own. If there is no such equal progress in other nations, then the industrial gain sought for the working classes of this country by a shorter day cannot be obtained, though any special class or classes of workers may be relieved of excessive toil at the expense of the community as a whole. Government employés, and that large number of workers who cannot be brought into direct competition with foreign labour, can receive the same wages for shorter hours, provided the public is willing to pay a higher price for their protected labour.

In conclusion, it may be well to add that the economic

difficulties which beset this question cannot be lightly set aside by an assertion that the same difficulties were raised by economists against earlier factory legislation, and that experience has shown that they may be safely disregarded. It is impossible to say how far the introduction of humane restrictions upon the exploitation of cheap human labour has affected the aggregate production of wealth in England. It has not prevented the growth of our trade, but very possibly it has checked the rate of growth. If the mere accumulation of material wealth, regardless alike of the mode of production or of the distribution, be regarded as the industrial goal, it is quite conceivable that a policy of utter *laissez faire* might be the best means of securing that end. Although healthy and happy workers are more efficient than the half-starved and wholly degraded beings who slaved in the uninspected factories and mines during the earlier period of the factory system, and still slave in the sweater's den, it may still be to the interest of employers to pay starvation wages for relatively inefficient work, rather than pay high wages for a shorter day's work to more efficient workers. It is to the capitalist a mere sum in arithmetic; and we cannot predict that the result will always turn in favour of humanity and justice.

At the same time, even if it is uncertain whether a shorter working day could be secured without a fall of wages, it is still open to advocates of a shorter working day to urge that it is worth while to purchase leisure at such a price. If a shorter working day could cure or abate the evil of "the unemployed," and help to raise the industrial condition of the low-skilled workers, the community might well afford to pay the cost.

CHAPTER VII.

OVER-SUPPLY OF LOW-SKILLED LABOUR.

§ 1. Restatement of the "Low-skilled Labour" Question.— Our inquiry into Factory Legislation and Trade Unionism as cures for sweating have served to emphasize the economic nature of the disease, the over-supply of low-skilled labour. Factory legislation, while it may abate many of the symptoms of the disease, cannot directly touch the centre of the malady, low wages, though by securing publicity it may be of indirect assistance in preventing the payment of wages which public opinion would condemn as insufficient for a decent livelihood. Trade Unionism as an effective agent in securing the industrial welfare of workers, is seen to rest upon the basis of restriction of labour supply, and its total effectiveness is limited by the fact that each exercise of this restriction in the interest of a class of workers weakens the position of the unemployed who are seeking work. The industrial degradation of the "sweated" workers arises from the fact that they are working surrounded by a pool of unemployed or superfluous supply of labour. So long as there remains this standing pool of excessive labour, it is difficult to see how the wages of low unskilled workers can be materially raised. The most intelligent social reformers are naturally directing their attention to the question, how to drain these lowlands of labour of the superfluous supply, or in other words to keep down the population of the low-skilled working class. Among the many population drainage schemes, the following deserve close attention—

§ 2. Checks on growth of population.—We need not discuss in its wider aspect the question whether our population tends to increase faster than the means of subsistence. Disciples of Malthus, who urge the growing pressure of population on the food supply, are sometimes told that so far as this argument applies to England, the growth of wealth is faster than the growth of population, and that as modern facilities for exchange enable any quantity of this wealth to be transferred into food and other necessaries, their alarm is groundless. Now these rival contentions have no concern for us. We are interested not in the pressure of the whole population upon an actual or possible food supply, but with the pressure of a certain portion of that population upon a relatively fixed supply of work. It is approximately true to say that at any given time there exists a certain quality of unskilled or low-skilled work to be done. If there are at hand just enough workers to do it, the wages will be sufficiently high to allow a decent standard of living. If, on the other hand, there are present more than enough workers willing to do the work, a number of them must remain without work and wages, while those who are employed get the lowest wages they will consent to take. Thus it will seem of prime importance to keep down the population of low-skilled workers to the point which leaves a merely nominal margin of superfluous labour. The Malthusian question has in its modern practical aspect narrowed down to this. The working classes by abstinence from early or improvident marriages, or by the exercise of moral restraints after marriage can, it is urged, check that tendency of the working population to outgrow the increase of the work for which they compete. There can be no doubt that the more intelligent classes of skilled labourers have already profited by this consideration, and as education and intelligence are more widely diffused, we may expect these prudential checks on "over-population" will operate with increased effect among the whole body of workers. But precisely because these checks are moral and reasonable, they must be of very slow acceptance among that class whose industrial condition forms a stubborn barrier to moral and intellectual progress. Those who would gain most by the practice of prudential checks, are least capable of practising them. The ordinary "labourer" earns full wages as soon as he attains manhood's strength; he is as able to support a wife and family at twenty as he will ever be; indeed he is more so, for while he is young his work is more regular, and less liable to interruption by ill-health. The reflection that an early marriage means the probability of a larger family, and that a large family helps to keep wages low, cannot at present be expected to make a deep impression upon the young unskilled labourer. The value of restraint after marriage could probably be inculcated with more effect, because it would appeal more intelligibly to the immediate interest of the labourer. But it is to the growing education and intelligence of women, rather than to that of men, that we must look for a recognition of the importance of restraint on early marriages and large families.

§ 3. The "Emigration" Remedy.—The most direct and obvious drainage scheme is by emigration. If there are more workers than there is work for them to do, why not remove those who are not wanted, and put them where there is work to do? The thing sounds very simple, but the simplicity is somewhat delusive. The old *laissez faire* political economist would ask, "Why, since labour is always moving towards the place where it can be most profitably employed, is it necessary to do anything but let it flow? Why should the State or philanthropic people busy themselves about the matter? If labour is not wanted in one place, and is wanted in another, it will and must leave the one place and go to the other. If you assist the process by compulsion, or by any artificial aid, you may be removing the wrong people, or you may be removing them to the wrong place." Now the reply to the main *laissez faire* position is conclusive. Just as water, though always tending to find its own level, does not actually find it when it is dammed up in some pool by natural or artificial earthworks, so labour stored in the persons of poor and ignorant men and women is not in fact free to seek the place of most profitable employment.

The highlands of labour are drained by this natural flow; even the strain of competition in skilled hand-labour finds sensible relief by the voluntary emigration of the more adventurous artisans, but the poor low-skilled workers suffer here again by reason of their poverty: no natural movement can relieve the plethora of labour-power in low-class employments. The fluidity of low-skilled labour seldom exceeds the power of moving from one town to a neighbouring town, or from a country district to the nearest market towns, or to London in search of work. If the lowlands are to be drained at all, it must be done by an artificial system. Now all such systems are in fact open to the mistakes mentioned above. If we look too exclusively to the requirements of new colonies, and the opportunities of work they present, we may be induced to remove from England a class of men and women whose services we can ill afford to lose, and who are not in any true sense superfluous labour. To assist sturdy and shrewd Scotch farmers, or a body of skilled artisans thrown out of work by a temporary trade depression, to transfer themselves and their families to America or Australia, is a policy the net advantage of which is open to grave doubt. Of course by removing any body of workers you make room for others, but this fact does not make it a matter of indifference which class is removed. On the other hand, if we look exclusively to the interests of the whole mass of labour in England, we should probably be led to assist the emigration of large bodies of the lowest and least competent workers. This course, though doubtless for the advantage of the low class labour, directly relieved, is detrimental to the interest of the new country, which is flooded with inefficient workers, and confers little benefit upon these workers themselves, since they are totally incapable of making their way in a new country. The reckless drafting off of our social failures into new lands is a criminal policy, which has been only too rife in the State-aided emigration of the past, and which is now rendered more and more difficult each year by the refusal of foreign lands to receive our "wreckage." Here, then, is the crux of emigration.

125

The class we can best afford to lose, is the class our colonies and foreign nations can least afford to take, and if they consent to receive them they only assume the burden we escape. The age of loose promiscuous pauper emigration has gone by. If we are to use foreign emigration as a mode of relief for our congested population in the future, it will be on condition that we select or educate our colonists before we send them out. Whether the State or private organizations undertake the work, our colonizing process must begin at home. The necessity of dealing directly with our weak surplus population of low-skilled workers is gaining more clear recognition every year, as the reluctance to interfere with the supposed freedom of the subject even where the subject is "unfree" is giving way before the urgency of the situation.

§ 4. **Mr. Charles Booth's "Drainage Scheme."**—The terrible examples our history presents to us of the effects of unwise poor law administration, rightly enjoin the strictest caution in contemplating new experiments. But the growing recognition of the duty of the State to protect its members who are unable to protect themselves, and to secure fair opportunities of self-support and self-improvement, as well as the danger of handing over their protection to the conflicting claims of private and often misguided philanthropy, is rapidly gaining ground against the advocates of *laissez faire*. It is beginning to be felt that the State cannot afford to allow the right of private social experiment on the part of charitable organizations. The relief of destitution has for centuries been recognized as the proper business of the State. Our present poor law practically fails to relieve the bulk of the really destitute. Even were it successful it would be doing nothing to prevent destitution. Since neither existing legislation nor the forces of private charity are competent to cope with the evils of "sweating," engendered by an excess of low-class labour, it is probable that the pressure of democratic government will make more and more in favour of some large new experiment of social drainage. In view of this it may not be out of place to describe briefly two schemes proposed by private students of the problem of poverty.

Mr. Charles Booth, recognizing that the superfluity of cheap inefficient labour lies at the root of the matter, suggests the removal of the most helpless and degraded class from the strain of a struggle which is fatal not merely to themselves, but to the class immediately above them. The reason for this removal is given as follows—

"To effectually deal with the whole of class B—for the State to nurse the helpless and incompetent as we in our own families nurse the old, the young, and the sick, and provide for those who are not competent to provide for themselves—may seem an impossible undertaking; but nothing less than this will enable self-respecting labour to obtain its full remuneration, and the nation its raised standard of life. The difficulties, which are certainly great, do not consist in the cost. As it is, these unfortunate people cost the community one way or another considerably more than they contribute. I do not refer solely to the fact that they cost the State more than they pay directly or indirectly in taxes. I mean that altogether, ill-paid and half-starved as they are, they consume, or waste, or have expended on them, more wealth than they produce."

Mr. Booth would remove the "very poor," and plant them in industrial communities under proper government supervision.

"Put practically, my idea is that these people should be allowed to live as families in industrial groups, planted wherever land and building materials were cheap; being well-housed and well-warmed, and taught, trained, and employed from morning to night on work, indoors or out, for themselves, or on Government account."

The Government should provide material and tools, and having the people entirely on its hands, get out of them what it can. Wages should be paid at a "fair proportionate rate," so as to admit comparison of earnings of the different communities, and of individuals. The commercial deficit involved in the scheme should be borne by the State. This expansion of our poor law policy, for it is nothing more, aims less at the reformation and improvement of the class taken under its charge, than at the relief which would be afforded to the classes who suffered from their competition in the industrial struggle. What it amounts to is the removal of the mass of unemployed. The difficulties involved in such a scheme are, as Mr. Booth admits, very grave.

The following points especially deserve attention—

1. Since it is not conceivable that compulsion should be brought to bear in the selection and removal out of the ordinary industrial community of those weaker members whose continued struggle is considered undesirable, it is evident that the industrial colonies must be recruited out of volunteers. It will thus become a large expansion of the present workhouse system. The eternal dilemma of the poor law will be present there. On the one hand, if, as seems likely, the degradation and disgrace attaching to the workhouse is extended to the industrial colony, it will fail to attract the more honest and deserving among the "very poor," and to this extent will fail to relieve the struggling workers of their competition. On the other hand, if the condition of the "industrial colonist" is recognized as preferable to that of the struggling free competitor, it must in some measure act as a premium upon industrial failure, checking the output of energy and the growth of self-reliance in the lower ranks of the working classes. No scheme for the relief of poverty is wholly free from this difficulty; but there is danger that the State colony of Mr. Booth would, if it were successful as a mode of "drainage," be open to it in no ordinary degree.

2. Closely related to this first difficulty is the fact that Mr. Booth provides no real suggestion for a process of discrimination in the treatment of our social failures, which shall distinguish the failure due directly to deep-seated vice of character and habit, from the failure due to unhappy chance or the fault of others. Difficult, almost impossible, as such discrimination between deserving and undeserving is, it is felt that any genuine reform of

our present poor law system demands that some attempt in this direction should be made. We must try to distinguish curable from incurable cases, and we must try to cure the former while we preserve society from the contamination of the latter. The mere removal of a class of "very poor" will not suffice.

Since however the scheme of Mr. C. Booth does not proceed beyond the stage of a suggested outline of treatment, it is not fair or profitable to press close criticism. It is, however, a fact of some significance that one who has brought such close study to bear upon the problem of poverty should arrive at the conclusion that "Thorough interference on the part of the State with the lives of a small fraction of the population, would tend to make it possible, ultimately, to dispense with any Socialistic interference in the lives of all the rest."[33]

§ 5. Proposed remedies for "Unemployment."—In discussing methods of dealing with "the unemployed," who represent an "over-supply" of labour at a given time, it is often found convenient to distinguish the temporary "unemployment" due to fluctuations rising from the nature of certain trades, and the permanent unemployment or half employment of large numbers of the least efficient town workers. The fluctuations in employment due to changes of season, as in the building trades, and many branches of dock labour, or to changes of fashion, as in the silk and "fancy" woollen trade, or to temporary changes in the field of employment caused by a transformation of industrial processes, are direct causes of a considerable quantity of temporary unemployment. To these must be added the unemployment represented by the interval between the termination of one job and the beginning of another, as in the building trades. Lastly, the wider fluctuations of general trade seem to impose a character of irregularity upon trade, so that the modern System of industry will not work without some unemployed margin, some reserve of labour.

These irregularities and leakages seem to explain why, at any given time, a certain considerable number of fairly efficient and willing workmen may be out of work. It is often urged that this class of "unemployed" must be regarded as quite distinct from the superfluity of low-skilled and inefficient workers found in our towns, and that the two classes present different problems for solution. The character of the "chronic" class of unemployed makes the problem appear to be, not one of economic readjustment, but rather of training and education. But this appearance is deceptive. The connection between the two kinds of "unemployment" is much closer than is supposed. The irregularity of the "season" and "fashion" trades, the periodic spells of bad trade, are continually engaged in degrading and deteriorating the physique, the morale, and the industrial efficiency of the weaker members of each trade: these weaklings are unable to maintain a steady and healthy standard of life under economic conditions which make work and wages irregular, and are constantly dropping out of the more skilled trades to swell the already congested low-skilled labour market. Every period of "depressed trade" feeds the pool of low-skilled labour from a hundred different channels. The connection between the two classes of "unemployed" is, therefore, a close and vital one. To drain off this pool would, in fact, be of little permanent use unless those irregularities of trade, which are constantly feeding it, are also checked.

Still less serviceable are those schemes of rescuing "the unemployed," which, in the very work of rescue, engender an economic force whose operation causes as much unemployment as it cures. A signal example of this futile system of social drainage has been afforded by certain experiments of the Salvation Army in their City Works and Farm Colony. The original draft of the scheme contained in the volume, *In Darkest England*, clearly recognized the advisability of keeping the bounty-fed products of the Salvation Colonies from competition in the market with the products of outside labour. The design was to withdraw from the competitive labour market certain members of "the unemployed," to train and educate them in efficient labour, and to apply this labour to capital provided out of charitable funds: the produce of this labour was to be consumed by the colonists themselves, who would thus become as far as possible self-supporting; in no case was it to be thrown upon the open market. As a matter of fact these sound, economic conditions of social experiment have been utterly ignored. Matches, firewood, furniture, etc. produced in the City factories have been thrown upon the open market. The Hadleigh Farm Colony, originally designed to give a thorough training in the arts of agriculture so as to educate its members for the Over Sea Colony, has devoted more and more attention to shoemaking, carpentering, and other special mechanical crafts, and less and less to the efficient cultivation of the soil; the boots, chairs, etc. being thrown in large quantities upon the open market. Moreover, the fruit and vegetables raised upon the Farm have been systematically placed upon the outside market. The result of such a line of conduct is evident. Suppose A is a carpenter thrown out of work because there are more carpenters than are required to turn out the current supply of chairs and tables at a profitable price; the Salvation Army takes A in hand, and provides him with capital upon which no interest need be paid. A's chairs, now thrown on the market, can undersell the chairs provided by B, C, D, his former trade competitors. Unless we suppose an increased demand for chairs, the result is that A's chairs displace those of B in the market, and B is thrown out of employment. Thus A, assisted by the Salvation Army, has simply taken B's work. If the Salvation Army now takes B in hand, it can engage him in useful work on condition that he takes away the work of C. If match-makers are thrown out of work by trade conditions, and the Salvation Army places them in a factory, and sells in the open market the matches which they make, the public which buys these matches abstains from buying the matches made by other firms, and these firms are thus prevented from employing as much labour as they would otherwise have done. No net increase of employment is caused by this action of the Salvation Army, and therefore they have done nothing towards the solution of the unemployed problem.

They have provided employment for certain known persons at the expense of throwing out of employment certain other unknown persons. Since those who are thrown out of work in the labour market are, on the average, inferior in character and industry to those who are kept in work, the effect of the Salvation Army policy is to substitute inferior for superior workers. The blind philanthropist may perhaps be excused for not seeing beyond his nose, and for ignoring "unseen" in favour of "seen" results. But General Booth was advised of the sound economic conditions of his experiment, and seemed to recognize the value of the advice. The defence of his action sometimes takes the form of a denial that the Salvation Army undersells outside produce in the market. Salvation matches are sold, it is said, rather above than below the ordinary price of matches. If this be true, it affords no answer to the objection raised above. The Salvation matches are bought by persons who would have bought other matches if they had not bought these, and if they choose to pay 3d. for Salvation matches instead of 2½d. for others, the effect of this action is still to take away employment from the 2½d. firm and give it to the Salvation firm. Indeed, it might be urged that a larger amount of unemployment is caused in this case, for persons who now pay 3d. for matches which they formerly bought for 2½d., will diminish their expenditure upon other commodities, and the result will be to diminish employment in those industries engaged in supplying these commodities. Here is another "unseen" result of fallacious philanthropy.

The inevitable result of the Salvation Army placing goods in the open market is to increase the supply relatively to the demand; in order that the larger supply may be sold prices must fall, and it makes no difference whether or no the Salvation Army takes the lead in reducing the price. If the fall of price enables the whole of the increased supply to be taken off at the lower price, then an increase of employment has been obtained in this trade, though, in this case, it should be remembered that in all probability the lower level of prices means a reduction of wages in the outside labour market. If the increased supply is not taken off at the lower prices, then the Salvation goods can only be sold on condition that some others remain unsold, employment of Salvationists thus displacing employment of other workers. The roundabout nature of much of this competition does not impair one whit the inevitability of this result.

This objection is applicable not only to the method of the Salvation Army, but to many other industrial experiments conducted on a philanthropic basis. Directly or indirectly bounty-fed labour is brought into competition with self-supporting labour to the detriment of the latter. It is sometimes sought to evade the difficulty by confining the produce which the assisted labour puts upon the open market to classes of articles which are not for the most part produced in this country, but which are largely imported from abroad. It is urged that although shoes and furniture and matches ought not to be produced by assisted labour for the outside market, it is permissible for an agricultural colony to replace by home products the large imports in the shape of cheese, fruit, bacon, poultry, etc., which we now receive from abroad. Those who maintain this position commonly fail to take into consideration the exports which go out from this country to pay for these imports. If this export trade is diminished the trades engaged in manufacturing the exported goods will suffer, and labour employed in these trades may be thrown out of employment. This objection may be met by showing that the goods formerly exported, or an equivalent quantity of other goods, will be demanded for the increased consumption of the labourers in the agricultural colony. This is a valid answer if the home consumption rises sufficiently to absorb the goods formerly exported to pay for agricultural imports. But even where this just balance is maintained, allowance must be made for some disturbance of established trades owing to the fact that the new demand created at home will probably be for different classes of articles from those which formed the exports now displaced. The safest use of assisted labour, where the products are designed for the open market, is in the production of articles for which there is a steadily growing demand within this country. Even in this case the utmost care should be exercised to prevent the products of assisted labour from so depressing prices as to injure the wages of outside labour engaged in similar productions.

Since the existence of an unemployed class who are unemployed because they are unable, not because they are unwilling, to get work, is proof of an insufficiency of employment, it is apparent that nothing is of real assistance which does not increase the net amount of employment. Since the amount of employment is determined by, and varies with, the consumption of the community, the only sure method of increasing the amount of employment is by raising the standard of consumption for the community. Where, as is common in times of trade depression, unemployment of labour is attended by unemployment of capital, this joint excess of the two requisites of production is only to be explained by the low standard of consumption of the community. Since the working-classes form a vast majority of the community, and their standard of consumption is low compared with that of the upper classes, it is to a progressive standard of comfort among the workers that we must look for a guarantee of increasing employment. It may be urged that the luxurious expenditure of the rich provides as much employment as the more necessary expenditure of the poor. But, setting aside all considerations of the inutility or noxious character of luxury, there is one vital difference between the employment afforded in the two cases. The demand for luxuries is essentially capricious and irregular, and this irregularity must always be reflected in the employment of the trades which supply them. On the other hand, a general rise in the standard of comfort of the workers creates an increased demand of a steady and habitual kind, the new elements of consumption belonging to the order of necessaries or primary comforts become ingrained in the habits of large classes of consumers, and the employment they afford is regular and reliable. When this simple principle is once clearly grasped by social reformers, it will enable them to see that the only effective remedy for unemployment lies in a general policy of social and economic reform, which aims at placing a larger and larger proportion of the "consuming power" of the community in the hands of those who, having received it as the earnings of their effort, will learn to use it in building up a higher standard of wholesome consumption.

CHAPTER VIII.

———————————————

THE INDUSTRIAL
CONDITION OF WOMEN-WORKERS.

§ 1. The Number of Women engaged in Industrial Work.— The evils of "sweating" press more heavily on women workers than on men. It is not merely that women as "the weaker sex" suffer more under the same burden, but that their industrial burden is absolutely heavier than that of men. The causes and the meaning of this demand a special treatment.

The census returns for 1901 showed that out of 4,171,751 females engaged in occupations about 40½ per cent. were in domestic or other service, 38½ per cent. in manufactures, 7 per cent. in commerce, chiefly as shop-assistants, 4 per cent. in teaching, 3 per cent. in hotels, boarding-houses, etc., and 7 per cent. in other occupations.

The following table gives the groups of occupations in which more females are employed than males:—

Occupational Groups	Males	Females
Sick nurses, midwives, etc.	1,092	67,269
Teaching	61,897	172,873
Domestic service	124,263	1,690,686
Bookbinding: paper and stationery manufactures	42,644	64,210
Textile manufactures	492,175	663,222
Dress manufactures	336,186	689,956
————————		
	1,058,257	3,348,216
All other occupations	9,098,717	823,535
————————		
All occupations	10,156,974	4,171,751

The manufactures in which women have been gaining upon men are the textile and clothing trades in almost all branches, tobacco, printing, stationery, brushes, india-rubber, and foods.

§ 2. **Women's Wages.**—Turning now to women engaged in city industries, let us gauge their industrial condition by the tests of wages, hours of labour, sanitary conditions, regularity of employment

The following is a list of the average wages paid for different kinds of factory work in London.

Artificial flowers	8 to	12 shillings.
Bookbinding	9 "	11 "
Boxmaking	8 "	16 "
Brushes	8 "	15 "
Caps	8 "	16 "
Collars	11 "	15 "
Confectionery	8 "	14 "
Corsets	8 "	16 "
Fur-sewing	7 "	14 "

Fur-sewing in winter	4 "	7 "
Matches	8 "	13 "
Rope	8 "	11 "
Umbrellas	10 "	18 "

These are ordinary wages. Very good or industrious workers are said to get in some cases 20 per cent, more; unskilful or idle workers less.

It must be borne in mind that these sums represent a full week's work. The importance of this qualification will appear presently.

It is obvious at a glance that these wages are for the most part considerably lower than those paid for any regular form of male labour. But there is another fact which adds to the significance of this. Skilled labour among men is much more highly paid than unskilled labour. Among women's industries this is not the case to any great extent. Skilled work like that of book-folding is paid no higher than the almost unskilled work of the jam or match girl. This is said to be due partly to the fact that the lower kinds of work are done by girls and women who are compelled to support themselves, while the higher class is done by women partly kept by husband or father, partly to the pride taken in the performance of more skilled work, and the reluctance to mingle with women belonging to a lower stratum of society, which prevents the wages of the various kinds of work from being determined by free economic competition. A bookbinding girl would sooner take lower wages than engage in an inferior class of work which happened to rise in the market price of its labour. But whatever the causes may be, the fact cannot be disputed that the lower rates of wages extend over a larger proportion of women workers.

Again, the wages quoted above refer to workers in factories. But only three women's trades of any importance are managed entirely in factories, the cigar, confectionery, and matchmaking[34] trades. In many of the other trades part of the work is done in factories, part is let out to sweaters, or to women who work at their own homes. Many of the clothing trades come under this class, as for example, the tie-making, trimmings, corset-making trades. The employers in these trades are able to play the out-doors workers against the indoors workers, so as to keep down the wages of both to a minimum. The "corset" manufacture is fairly representative of these trades. The following list gives the per-centage of workers receiving various sums for "indoors" i.e. "factory" work.

S.	S. S.	S. S.	S. S.	S. S.	S.
Under 4	3 — 6	8 — 10	10 — 12	12 — 15	Over 15
2.94 P.C.	50 P.C.	2.94 P.C.	5.9 P.C.	14.7 P.C.	22.52 P.C.

Outdoor workers earn from 6s. to 12s., but where more than 10s. is earned, the woman is generally assisted by one or more of her children. Generally speaking, the most miserably paid work is that in trades where most of the work is done by out-door workers. Such is the lowest stratum of the "vest and trousers" trade, where English women undertake work rejected by the lowest class of Jew workers, and the shirt-making trade, which, in the opinion of the Lords' Committee, "does not appear to afford subsistence to those who have no other employment." In these and other trades of the lowest order, 6s. a week is a tolerably common wage for a work-woman of fair skill to net after a hard week's work, and there are many individual cases where the wage falls far below this mark.

It is true that the work for which the lowest wages are paid is often that of learners, or of inefficient work-women; but while this may be a satisfactory "economic" explanation, it does not mitigate the terrible significance of the fact that many women are dependent on such work as their sole opportunity of earning an honest livelihood.

§ 3. **Irregularity of Employment.**—As the wages of women are lower than those of men, so they suffer more from irregularity of employment. There are two special reasons for this.

α. Many trades in which women are employed, depend largely upon the element of Season. The confectionery trade, one of the most important, employs twice as many hands in the busy season as in the slack season. Match-makers have a slack season, in which many of them sell flowers, or go "hopping." Laundry work is largely "season" work. Fur-sewing is perhaps the worst example of the terrible effect of irregular work taken with low wages. "For several months in the year the fur-sewers have either no work, or earn about 3s. or 4s. a week, and many of these work in overcrowded insanitary workshops in the season. Fur-sewing is the worst paid industry in the East End, with absolutely no exceptions."[35]

β. Fluctuations in fashion affect many women's trades; in particular, the "ornamental" clothing trades, e.g. furs, feathers, trimmings, etc.

Employers in these slack times prefer generally to keep on the better hands (on lower wages), and to dismiss the inferior hands. These "natural" fluctuations, added to ordinary trade irregularities, favour the employment of "outdoor" workers in sweaters' dens or at home, and require in these trades, as conducted at present, the existence of an enormous margin of "casual" workers. These two chief factors in the "sweating" problem, sub-contract and irregular home-work, are far more prevalent in female industries than in male.

§ 4. **Hours of Labour in Women's Trades.**—The Factory Act is supposed to protect women engaged in industrial work from excessive hours of labour, by setting a limit of twelve hours to the working day, including an interval of two hours for meals.

But passing over the fact that a dispensation is granted, enabling women to be employed for fourteen hours during certain times, there is the far more important consideration that most employments of women wholly escape the operation of the Factory Act. In part this is due to the difficulty of enforcing the Act in the case of sweating workshops, many of which are unknown to inspectors, while others habitually break the law and escape the penalty. Again, the Act does not and cannot be made to apply to a large class of small domestic workshops. When the dwelling-room is also the work-room, it is impossible to enforce by any machinery of law, close limitation of hours of labour. Something may be done to extend the arm of the law over small workshops; but the worst form of out-work, that voluntarily undertaken by women in their own homes, cannot be thus put down. Nothing short of a total prohibition of outwork imposed on employers would be effectual here. Lastly, there are many large employments not subject to the Factory Act, where the economic power of the employer over weak employees is grossly abused. One of the worst instances is that of the large laundries, where women work enormously long hours during the season, and are often engaged for fifteen or sixteen hours on Fridays and Saturdays. The whole class of shop-assistants are worked excessive hours. Twelve and fourteen hours are a common shop day, and frequently the figure rises to sixteen hours. Restaurants and public-houses are perhaps the greatest offenders. The case of shop-assistants is most aggravated, for these excessive hours of labour are wholly waste time; a reduction of 25 or even of 50 per cent in the shopping-day, reasonably adjusted to the requirements of classes and localities, would cause no diminution in the quantity of sales effected, nor would it cause any appreciable inconvenience to the consuming public.

§ 5. **Sanitary Conditions.**—Seeing that a larger proportion of women workers are occupied in the small workshops or in their own overcrowded homes, it is obvious that the fourth count of the "sweating" charge, that of unsanitary conditions of work, applies more cruelly to them than to men. Their more sedentary occupations, and the longer hours they work in many cases outside the operation of the Factory Act, makes the evils of overcrowding, bad ventilation, bad drainage, etc., more detrimental to the health of women than of men workers.

§ 6. **Special Burdens incident on Women.**—We have now applied the four chief heads of the "sweating" disease—low wages, long hours, irregular employment, unsanitary conditions—to women's work, and have seen that the absolute pressure in each case is heavier on the weaker sex.

But in estimating the industrial condition of women, there are certain other considerations which must not be left out of sight.

To many women-workers, the duties of maternity and the care of children, which in a civilized human society ought to secure for them some remission from the burden, of the industrial fight, are a positive handicap in the struggle for a livelihood. When a married woman or a widow is compelled to support herself and her family, the home ties which preclude her from the acceptance of regular factory work, tell fatally against her in the effort to earn a living. Married women, and others with home duties which cannot be neglected, furnish an almost illimitable field of casual or irregular labour. Not only is this irregular work worse paid than regular factory work, but its existence helps to keep up the pernicious system of "out-work" under which "sweating" thrives. The commercial competition of to-day positively trades upon the maternity of women-workers.

In estimating the quantity of work which falls to the lot of industrial women-workers, we must not forget to add to the wage-work that domestic work which few of them can wholly avoid, and which is represented by no wages. Looking at the problem in a broad human light, it is difficult to say which is the graver evil, the additional burden of the domestic work, so far as it is done, or the habitual neglect of it, where it is evaded. Here perhaps the former point of view is more pertinent. To the long hours of the factory-worker, or the shopwoman, we must often add the irksome duties which to a weary wife must make the return home a pain rather than a pleasure. When the industrial work is carried on at home the worries and interruptions of family life must always contribute to the difficulty and intensity of the toil, and tell upon the nervous system and the general health of the women-workers.

Other evils, incident on woman's industrial work, do not require elaboration, though their cumulative effect is often very real. Many women-workers, the locality of whose home depends on the work of their husband or father, are obliged to travel every day long distances to and from their work. The waste of time, the weariness, and sometimes the expense of 'bus or train thus imposed on them, is in thousands of cases a heavy tax upon their industrial life. Women working in factories, or taking work home, suffer also many wrongs by reason of their "weaker sex," and their general lack of trade organization. Unjust and arbitrary fines are imposed by harsh employers so as to filch a portion of their scanty earnings; their time is wasted by unnecessary delay in the giving out of work, or its inspection when finished; the brutality and insolence of male overseers is a common incident in their career. In a score of different ways the weakness of women injures them as competitors in the free fight for industrial work.

§ 7. **Causes of the Industrial Weakness of Women.**—This brief summary of the industrial condition of low-skilled women-workers will suffice to bring out the fact that the "sweating" question is even more a woman's question than a man's. The question which rises next is, Why do women as industrial workers suffer more than men?

In the first place, as the physically weaker sex, they do on the average a smaller quantity of work, and therefore receive lower wages. In certain kinds of work, where women do piece-work along with men, it is found that they get as high wages as men for the same quantity of work. The recent report upon Textile Industries establishes this fact so far as those trades are concerned. But this is not always, perhaps not in the majority of instances, the case. Women-workers do not, in many cases, receive the same wages which would be paid to men for doing the same work. Why is this? It is sometimes described as an unfair advantage taken of women because they are women. There is a male prejudice, it is urged, against women-workers, which prevents employers from paying them the wages they could and would pay to men.

Now this contention, so far as it refers to a sentimental bias, is not tenable. A body of women-workers, equally skilled with male workers, and as strongly organized, would be able to extract the same rate of wages in any trade. Everything depends upon the words "*as strongly organized.*" It is the general industrial weakness of the condition of most women-workers, and not a sex prejudice, which prevents them from receiving the wages which men might get, if the work the women do were left for male competition alone. An employer, as a rule, pays the lowest wages he can get the work done at. The real question we have to meet is this. Why can he get women who will consent to work at a lower rate than he could get men to work at? What peculiar conditions are there affecting women which will oblige them to accept work on lower terms than men?

Well, in the first place, the wage of a man can never fall much lower than will suffice to maintain at the minimum standard of comfort both himself and the average family he has to support. The minimum wage of the man, it is true, need not cover the full support of his family, because the wife or children will on the average contribute something to their maintenance. But the wage of the man must cover his own support, and part of the support of his family. This marks a rigid minimum wage for male labour; if competition tends to drive wages lower, the supply of labour is limited to unmarried males.

The case of woman is different. If she is a free woman her minimum wage will be what is required to support herself alone, and since a woman appears able to keep alive and in working condition on a lower scale of expenditure than man, the possible minimum wage for independent women-workers will be less than a single man would consent to work for, and considerably less than what a married man would require. But there are other economic causes more important than this which drag down women's wages.

Single women, working to support themselves, are subject to the constant competition of other women who are not dependent for their full livelihood on the wages they get, and who, if necessary, are often willing to take wages which would not keep them alive if they had no other source of income. The minimum wages which can be obtained for certain kinds of work may by this competition of "bounty-fed" labour be driven considerably below starvation point. This is no mere hypothesis. It will be obvious that the class of fur-sewers who, as we saw, earned while in full work from 4s. to 7s. in the winter months, and the lower grades of brush-makers and match-makers, to say nothing of the casual "out-workers," who often take for a whole week's work 3s. or 2s. 6d., cannot, and do not, live upon these earnings. They must either die upon them, as many in fact do, or else they must be assisted by other funds.

There are, at least, three classes of female workers whose competition helps to keep wages below the point of bare subsistence in the employments which they enter.

First, there are married women who in their eagerness to increase the family income, or to procure special comforts for themselves, are willing to work at what must be regarded as "uncommercial rates"; that is to say, for lower wages than they would be willing to accept if they were working for full maintenance. It is sometimes asserted that since these married women have not so strong a motive to secure work, they will not, and in fact do not, undersell, and bring down the rate of wages. But it must be admitted, firstly, that the very addition of their number to the total of competitors for low-skilled work, forces down, and keeps down, the price paid for that work; and secondly, that if they choose, they are enabled to underbid at any time the labour of women entirely dependent on themselves for support. The existence of this competition of married women must be regarded as one of the reasons why wages are low in women's employments.

Secondly, a large proportion of unmarried women live at home. Even if they pay their parents the full cost of their keep, they can live more cheaply than if they had to find a home for themselves. A large proportion, however, of the younger women are partly supported at the expense of their family, and work largely to provide luxuries in the shape of dress, and other ornamental articles. Many of them will consent to work long hours all week, for an incredibly low sum to spend on superfluities.

Thirdly, there is the competition of women assisted by charity, or in receipt of out-door poor relief. Sums paid by Boards of Guardians to widows with young children, or assistance given by charitable persons to aid women in distressed circumstances to earn a livelihood, will enable these women to get work by accepting wages which would have been impossible if they had not outside assistance to depend upon. It is thus possible that by assisting a thoroughly deserving case, you may be helping to drive down below starvation-point the wages of a class of workers.

Probably a large majority of women-workers are to some extent bounty-fed in one of these ways. In so far as they do receive assistance from one of these sources, enabling them to accept lower wages than they could otherwise have done, it should be clearly understood that they are presenting the difference between the commercial and the uncommercial price as a free gift to their employer, or in so far as competition will oblige him to lower his prices, to the public, which purchases the results of their work. But the most terrible effect of this uncommercial competition falls on that miserable minority of their sisters who have no such extra source of income, and who have to make the lower wages find clothes, and shelter for themselves, and perhaps a family of children. We hear a good deal about the jealousy of men, and the difficulties male Trade Unions have sometimes thrown in the way of women obtaining employment, which may seem to affect male interests. But though there is doubtless some ground for these complaints, it should be acknowledged that it is women who are the real enemies of women. Women's wages in the "sweating" trades are almost incredibly low, because there is an artificially large supply of women able and willing to take work at these low rates.

It will be possible to raise the wages in these low-paid employments only on condition that women will agree to refuse to undersell one another beyond a certain point. A restriction in what is called "freedom of competition" is the only direct remedy which can be applied by women themselves. If women could be induced to refuse to avail themselves of the terrible power conferred by these different forms of "bounty," their wages could not fall below that 9s. or 10s. which would be required to keep them alive, and would probably rise higher.

§ 8. **What Trade Unionism can do for them.**—A question which naturally rises now is, how far combination in the form of Trade Unionism can assist to raise the industrial condition of these women. The practical power wielded by male Unions we saw was twofold. Firstly, by restricting the supply of labour in their respective trades they raised its market price, i.e. wages. Secondly, they could extract better conditions from employers, by obliging the latter to deal with them as a single large body instead of dealing with them as a number of individuals. How far can women-workers effect these same ends by these same means?

Trade Unionism, so far as women are concerned, is yet in its infancy. In 1874, Mrs. Paterson established a society, now named the Women's Trades Union Provident League, to try and establish combination among women in their several trades. The first Union was that of women engaged in book-binding, formed in September 1874. Since then a considerable number of Unions have been formed among match-makers, dressmakers, milliners, mantle-makers, upholstresses, rope-makers, confectioners, box-makers, shirt-makers, umbrella-makers, brush-makers and others. Many of these have been formed to remedy some pressing grievance, or to secure some definite advance of wage, and in certain cases of skilled factory work where the women have maintained a steady front, as among the match-makers and the confectioners, considerable concessions have been won from employers. But the small scale and tentative character of most of these organizations do not yet afford any adequate test of what Unionism can achieve. The workers in a few factories here and there have formed a Union of, at the most, a few hundred workers. No large women's trade has yet been organized with anything approaching the size and completeness of the stronger men's Unions. Women Trade Unionists numbered 120,178 in 1901, and of these no less than 89.9 per cent were textile workers, whose Unions are mostly organized by and associated with male Unions.

There are several reasons why the growth of effective organization among women-workers must be slow. In the first place, as we have seen, a large proportion of their work is "out work" done at home or in small domestic workshops. Now labour organizations are necessarily strong and effective, in proportion as the labourers are thrown together constantly both in their work and in their leisure, have free and frequent opportunities of meeting and discussion, of educating a sense of comradeship and mutual confidence, which shall form a moral basis of unity for common industrial action. But to the majority of women-workers no such opportunities are open. Even the factory workers are for the most part employed in small groups, and are dispersed in their homes. Combination among the mass of home-workers or workers in small sweating establishments is almost impossible. The women's Unions have hitherto been successful in proportion as the trades are factory trades. Where endeavours have been made to organize East End shirt-makers, milliners, and others who work at home, very little has been achieved. In those trades where it is possible to give out an indefinite amount of the work to sub-contractors, or to workers to do at home, it seems impossible that any great results can be thus attained. Even in trades where part of the work is done in factories, the existence of reckless competition among unorganized out-workers can be utilized by unprincipled employers to destroy attempts at effective combination among their factory hands. The force of public opinion which may support an organization of factory workers by preventing outsiders from underselling, can have no effect upon the competition of home-workers, who bid in ignorance of their competitors, and bid often for the means of keeping life in themselves and their children. The very poverty of the mass of women-workers, the low industrial conditions, which Unionism seeks to relieve, form cruel barriers to the success of their attempts. The low physical condition, the chronic exhaustion produced by the long hours and fetid atmosphere in which the poorer workers live, crush out the human energy required for effective protest and combination. Moreover, the power to strike, and, if necessary, to hold out for a long period of time, is an essential to a strong Trade Union. Almost all the advantages won by women's Unions have been won by their proved capacity for holding out against employers. This is largely a matter of funds. It is almost impossible for the poorest classes of women-workers to raise by their own abstinence a fund which shall make their Union formidable. Their efforts where successful have been always backed by outside assistance. Even were there a close federation of Unions of various women's trades—a distant dream at present—the larger proportion of recipients of low wages among women-workers as compared with men would render their success more difficult.

§ 9. **Legislative Restriction and the force of Public Opinion.**—If Trade Unionism among women is destined to achieve any large result, it would appear that it will require to be supported by two extra-Union forces.

The first of these forces must consist of legislative restriction of "out-work." If all employers of women were compelled to provide factories, and to employ them there in doing that work at present done at home or in small and practically unapproachable workshops, several wholesome results would follow. The conditions of effective combination would be secured, public opinion would assist in securing decent wages, factory inspection would provide shorter hours and fair sanitary conditions, and last, not least, women whose home duties precluded them from full factory work would be taken out of the field of competition. Whether it would be possible to successfully crush the whole system of industrial "out-work" may be open to question; but it is certain that so long as, and in proportion as "out-work" is permitted, attempts on the part of women to raise their industrial condition by combination will be weak and unsuccessful. So long as "out-work" continues to be largely practised and unrestrained, competition sharpened by the action of married women and other irregular and "bounty-fed" labour, must keep down the price of women's work, not only for the out-workers themselves, but also for the factory workers. Nor is it possible to see how the system of "out-work" can be repressed or even restricted by any other force than legislation. So long as home-workers are "free" to offer, and employers to accept, this labour, it will continue to exist so long as it pays; it will pay so long as it is offered cheap enough; and it will be offered cheaply so long as the supply continues to bear the present relation to the demand.

But there is another force required to give any full effect to such extensions of the Factory Act as will crush private workshops, and either directly or indirectly prohibit out-work. The real reason, as we saw, why woman's wages were proportionately lower than man's, was the competition of a mass of women, able and willing to work at indefinitely low rates, because they were wholly or partly supported from other sources. Now legislation can hardly interfere to prevent this competition, but public opinion can. If the greater part of the industrial work now done by women at home were done in factories, this fact in itself would offer some restrictions to the competition of married women, which is so fatal to those who depend entirely upon their wages for a livelihood. But the gradual growth of a strong public opinion, fed by a clear perception of the harm married women do to their unsupported sisters by their competition, and directed towards the establishment of a healthy social feeling against the wage-earning proclivities of married women, would be a far more wholesome as well as a more potent method of interference than the passing of any law.

To interfere with the work of young women living at home, and supported in large part by their parents, would be impracticable even if it were desirable, although the competition of these conduces to the same lowering of women's wages. But the education of a strong popular sentiment against the propriety of the industrial labour of married women, would be not only practicable, but highly desirable. Such a public sentiment would not at first operate so stringently as to interfere in those exceptional cases where it seems an absolute necessity that the wife should aid by her home or factory work the family income. But a steady pressure of public opinion, making for the closer restriction of the wage-work of married women, would be of incomparable value to the movement to secure better industrial conditions for those women who are obliged to work for a living. A fuller, clearer realization of the importance of this subject is much needed at the present time. The industrial emancipation of women, favoured by the liberal sentiments of the age, has been eagerly utilized by enterprising managers of businesses in search of the cheapest labour. Not only women, but also children are enabled, owing to the nature of recent mechanical inventions which relieve the physical strain, but increase the monotony of labour, to make themselves useful in factories or home-work. Each year sees a large growth in the ranks of women-workers. Eager to earn each what she can, girls and wives alike rush into factory work, reckless of the fact that their very readiness to work tells against them in the amount of their weekly wages, and only goes to swell the dividends of the capitalist, or perhaps eventually to lower prices. The improving mechanism of our State School System assists this movement, by turning out every year a larger percentage of half-timers, crammed to qualify for wage-earners at the earliest possible period. Already in Lancashire and elsewhere, the labour of these thirteen-year-olders is competing with the labour of their fathers. The substitution of the "ring" for the "mule" in Lancashire mills, is responsible for the sight which may now be seen, of strong men lounging about the streets, supported by the earnings of their own children, who have undersold them in the labour market. The "ring" machine can be worked by a child, and can be learned in half an hour; that is the sole explanation of this deplorable phenomenon.

In the case of child-work, with its degrading consequences on the physical and mental health of the victim thus prematurely thrust into the struggle of life, legislation can doubtless do much. By raising the standard of education, and, if necessary, by an absolute prohibition of child-work, the State would be keeping well within the powers which the strictest individualist would assign to it, as it would be merely protecting the rising generation against the cupidity of parents and the encroachments of industrial competition.

The case of married women-workers is different. Better education of women in domestic work and the requirements of wifehood and motherhood; the growth of a juster and more wholesome feeling in the man, that he may refuse to demand that his wife add wage-work to her domestic drudgery; and above all, a clearer and more generally diffused perception in society of the value of healthy and careful provision for the children of our race, should build up a bulwark of public opinion, which shall offer stronger and stronger obstruction to the employment of married women, either outside or inside the home, in the capacity of industrial wage-earners. The satisfaction rightly felt in the ever wider opportunities afforded to unmarried women of earning an independent livelihood, and of using their abilities and energies in socially useful work, is considerably qualified by our perception of the injury which these new opportunities inflict upon our offspring and our homes. Surely, from the large standpoint of true national economy, no wiser use could be made of the vast expansion of the wealth-producing power of the nation under the reign of machinery, than to secure for every woman destined to be a wife and a mother, that relief from the physical strain of industrial toil which shall enable her to bring forth healthy offspring, and to employ her time and attention in their nurture, and in the ordering of a cleanly, wholesome, peaceful home life. So long as public opinion permits or even encourages women, who either are or will be mothers, to neglect the preparation for, and the performance of, the duties of domestic life and of maternity, by engaging in laborious and unhealthy industrial occupations, so long shall we pay the penalty in that physical and moral deterioration of the race which we have traced in low city life. How can the women of Cradley Heath engaged in wielding huge sledge-hammers, or carrying on their neck a hundredweight of chain for twelve or fourteen hours a day, in order to earn five or seven shillings a week, bear or rear healthy children? What "hope of our race" can we expect from the average London factory hand? What "home" is she capable of making for her husband and her children? The high death-rate of the "slum" children must be largely attributed to the fact that the women are factory workers first and mothers afterwards. Roscher, the German economist, assigns as the reason why the Jewish population of Prussia increases so much faster than the Christian, the fact that the Jewish mothers seldom go out of their own homes to work.[36] One of the chief social dangers of the age is the effect of industrial work upon the motherhood of the race. Surely, the first duty of society should be to secure healthy conditions for the lives of the young, so as to lay a firm physical foundation for the progress of the race.

This we neglect to do when we look with indifference or complacency upon the present phase of unrestricted competition in industrial work amongst women. So long as we refuse to insist, as a nation, that along with the growth of national wealth there shall be secured those conditions of healthy home life requisite for the sound, physical, moral, and intellectual growth of the young, at whatever cost of interference with so-called private liberty of action, we are rendering ourselves as a nation deliberately responsible for the continuance of that creature whose appearance gives a loud lie to our claim of civilization— the gutter child of our city streets. Thousands of these children, as we well know, the direct product of economic maladjustment, grow up every year—in our great cities to pass from babyhood into the street arab, afterwards to become what they may, tramp, pauper, criminal, casual labourer, feeble-bodied, weak-minded, desolate creatures, incapable of strong, continuous effort at any useful work. These are the children who have never known a healthy home. With that poverty which compels mothers to be wage-earners, lies no small share of the responsibility of this sin against society and moral progress. It is true that no sudden general prohibition of married woman's work would be feasible. But it is surely to be hoped that with every future rise in the wages and industrial position of male wage-earners, there may be a growing sentiment in favour of a restriction of industrial work among married women.

CHAPTER IX.

MORAL ASPECTS OF POVERTY.

§ 1. "Moral" View of the Causes of Poverty.—Our diagnosis of "sweating" has regarded poverty as an industrial disease, and we have therefore concerned ourselves with the examination of industrial remedies, factory legislation, Trade Unionism, and restrictions of the supply of unskilled labour. It may seem that in doing this we have ignored certain important moral factors in the problem, which, in the opinion of many, are all important. Until quite recently the vast majority of those philanthropic persons who interested themselves in the miserable conditions of the poor, paid very slight attention to the economic aspect of poverty, and never dreamed of the application of economic remedies. It is not unnatural that religions and moral teachers engaged in active detailed work among the poor should be so strongly impressed by the moral symptoms of the disease as to mistake them for the prime causes. "It is a fact apparent to every thoughtful man that the larger portion of the misery that constitutes our Social Question arises from idleness, gluttony, drink, waste, indulgence, profligacy, betting, and dissipation." These words of Mr. Arnold White express the common view of those philanthropists who do not understand what is meant by "the industrial system," and of the bulk of the comfortable classes when they are confronted with the evils of poverty as disclosed in "the sweating system." Intemperance, unthrift, idleness, and inefficiency are indeed common vices of the poor. If therefore we could teach the poor to be temperate, thrifty, industrious, and efficient, would not the problem of poverty be solved? Is not a moral remedy instead of an economic remedy the one to be desired? The question at issue here is a vital one to all who earnestly desire to secure a better life for the poor. This "moral view" has much to recommend it at first sight. In the first place, it is a "moral" view, and as morality is admittedly the truest and most real end of man, it would seem that a moral cure must be more radical and efficient than any merely industrial cure. Again, these "vices" of the poor, drink, dirt, gambling, prostitution, &c., are very definite and concrete maladies attaching to large numbers of individual cases, and visibly responsible for the misery and degradation of the vicious and their families. Last, not least, this aspect of poverty, by representing the condition of the poor to be chiefly "their own fault," lightens the sense of responsibility for the "well to do." It is decidedly the more comfortable view, for it at once flatters the pride of the rich by representing poverty as an evidence of incompetency, salves his conscience when pricked by the contrast of the misery around him, and assists him to secure his material interests by adopting an attitude of stern repression towards large industrial or political agitations in the interests of labour, on the ground that "these are wrong ways of tackling the question."

§ 2. "Unemployment" and the Vices of the Poor.—The question is this, Can the poor be moralized, and will that cure Poverty? To discuss this question with the fullness it deserves is here impossible, but the following considerations will furnish some data for an answer—

In the first place, it is very difficult to ascertain to what extent drink, vice, idleness, and other personal defects are actually responsible for poverty in individual cases. There is, however, reason to believe that the bulk of cases of extreme poverty and destitution cannot be traced to these personal vices, but, on the other hand, that they are attributable to industrial causes for which the sufferer is not responsible. The following is the result of a careful analysis of 4000 cases of "very poor" undertaken by Mr. Charles Booth. These are grouped as follows according to the apparent causes of distress—

- 4 per cent, are "loafers."
- 14 " " are attributed to drink and thriftlessness.
- 27 " " are due to illness, large families, or other misfortunes.
- 55 " " are assigned to "questions of employment."

Here, in the lowest class of city poor, moral defects are the direct cause of distress in only 18 per cent. of the cases, though doubtless they may have acted as contributory or indirect causes in a larger number.

In the classes just above the "very poor," 68 per cent. of poverty is attributed to "questions of employment," and only 13 per cent. to drink and thriftlessness. In the lowest parts of Whitechapel drink figures very slightly, affecting only 4 per cent. of the very poor, and 1 per cent. of the poor, according to Mr. Booth. Even applied to a higher grade of labour, a close investigation of facts discloses a grossly exaggerated notion of the sums spent in drink by city workers in receipt of good wages. A careful inquiry into the expenditure of a body of three hundred Amalgamated Engineers during a period of two years, yielded an average of 1s. 9d. per week spent on drink.

So, too, in the cases brought to the notice of the Lords' Committee, drink and personal vices do not play the most important part. The Rev. S. A. Barnett, who knows East London so well, does not find the origin of poverty in the vices of the poor. Terrible as are the results of drunkenness, impurity, unthrift, idleness, disregard of sanitary rules, it is not possible, looking fairly at the facts, to regard these as the main sources of poverty. If we are not carried away by the spirit of some special fanaticism, we shall look upon these evils as the natural and necessary accessories of the struggle for a livelihood, carried on under the industrial conditions of our age and country. Even supposing it were demonstrable that a much larger proportion of the cases of poverty and misery were the direct consequence of these moral and sanitary vices of the poor, we should not be justified in concluding that moral influence and education were the most effectual cures, capable of direct application. It is indeed highly probable that the "unemployed" worker is on the average morally and industrially inferior to the "employed," and from the individual point of view this inferiority is often responsible for his non-employment. But this only means that differences of moral and industrial character determine what particular individuals shall succeed or fail in the fight for work and wages. It by no means follows that if by education we could improve all these moral and industrial weaklings they could obtain steady employment without displacing others. Where an over-supply of labour exists, no remedy which does not operate either by restricting the supply or increasing the demand for labour can be effectual.

§ 3. **Civilization ascends from Material to Moral.**—The life of the poorest and most degraded classes is impenetrable to the highest influences of civilization. So long as the bare struggle for continuance of physical existence absorbs all their energies, they cannot be civilized. The consideration of the greater intrinsic worth of the moral life than the merely physical life, must not be allowed to mislead us. That which has the precedence in value has not the precedence in time. We must begin with the lower life before we can ascend to the higher. As in the individual the *corpus sanum* is rightly an object of earlier solicitude in education than the *mens sana*, though the latter may be of higher importance; so with the progress of a class. We cannot go to the lowest of our slum population and teach them to be clean, thrifty, industrious, steady, moral, intellectual, and religious, until we have first taught them how to secure for themselves the industrial conditions of healthy physical life. Our poorest classes have neither the time, the energy, or the desire to be clean, thrifty, intellectual, moral, or religious. In our haste we forget that there is a proper and necessary order in the awakening of desires. At present our "slum" population do not desire to be moral and intellectual, or even to be particularly clean. Therefore these higher goods must wait, so far as they are dependent on the voluntary action of the poor. What these people do want is better food, and more of it; warmer clothes; better and surer shelter; and greater security of permanent employment on decent wages. Until we can assist them to gratify these "lower" desires, we shall try in vain to awaken "higher" ones. We must prepare the soil of a healthy physical existence before we can hope to sow the moral seed so as to bring forth fruit. Upon a sound physical foundation alone can we build a high moral and spiritual civilization.

Moral and sanitary reformers have their proper sphere of action among those portions of the working classes who have climbed the first rounds in the ladder of civilization, and stand on tolerably firm conditions of material comfort and security. They cannot hope at present to achieve any great success among the poorest workers. The fact must not be shirked that in preaching thrift, hygiene, morality, and religion to the dwellers in the courts and alleys of our great cities, we are sowing seed upon a barren ground. Certain isolated cases of success must not blind us to this truth. Take, for example, thrift. It is not possible to expect that large class of workers who depend upon irregular earnings of less than 18s. a week to set by anything for a rainy day. The essence of thrift is regularity, and regularity is to them impossible. Even supposing their scant wage was regular, it is questionable whether they would be justified in stinting the bodily necessities of their families by setting aside a portion which could not in the long run suffice to provide even a bare maintenance for old age or disablement. To say this is not to impugn the value of thrift in maintaining a character of dignity and independence in the worker; it is simply to recognize that valuable as these qualities are, they must be subordinated to the first demands of physical life. Those who can save without encroaching on the prime necessaries of life ought to save; but there are still many who cannot save, and these are they whom the problem of poverty especially concerns. The saying of Aristotle, that "it is needful first to have a maintenance, and then to practise virtue," does not indeed imply that we *ought* to postpone practising the moral virtues until we have secured ourselves against want, but rather means that before we can live well we *must* first be able to live at all.

Precisely the same is true of the "inefficiency" of the poor. Nothing is more common than to hear men and women, often incapable themselves of earning by work the money which they spend, assigning as the root of poverty the inefficiency of the poor. It is quite true that the "poor" consist for the most part of inefficient workers. It would be strange if it were not so. How shall a child of the slums, ill-fed in body and mind, brought up in the industrial and moral degradation of low city life, without a chance of learning how to use hands or head, and to acquire habits of steady industry, become an efficient workman? The conditions under which they grow up to manhood and womanhood preclude the possibility of efficiency. It is the bitterest portion of the lot of the poor that they are deprived of the opportunity of learning to work well. To taunt them with their incapacity, and to regard it as the cause of poverty, is nothing else than a piece of blind insolence. Here and there an individual may be to blame for neglected opportunities; but the "poor" as a class have no more chance under present conditions of acquiring "efficiency" than of attaining to refined artistic taste, or the culminating Christian virtue of holiness. Inefficiency is one of the worst and most degrading aspects of poverty; but to regard it as the leading cause is an error fatal to a true understanding of the problem.

We now see why it is impossible to seriously entertain the claim of Co-operative Production as a direct remedy for poverty. The success of Co-operative schemes depends almost entirely upon the presence of high moral and intellectual qualities in those co-operating—trust, patience, self restraint, and obedience combined with power of organization, skill, and business enterprise. These qualities are not yet possessed by our skilled artisan class to the extent requisite to enable them to readily succeed in productive co-operation; how can it be expected then that low-skilled inefficient labour should exhibit them? The enthusiastic co-operator says we must educate them up to the requisite moral and intellectual level. The answer is, that it is impossible to apply such educating influences effectually, until we have first placed them on a sound physical basis of existence; that is to say, until we have already cured the worst form of the malady. From whatever point we approach this question we are driven to the conclusion that as the true cause of the disease is an industrial one, so the earliest remedies must be rather industrial than moral or educational.

§ 4. **Effects of Temperance and Technical Education.**— Again, we are by no means justified in leaping to the conclusion that if we could induce workers to become more sober, more industrious, or more skilful, their industrial condition would of necessity be improved to a corresponding extent. If we can induce an odd farm-labourer here and there to give up his "beer," he and his family are no doubt better off to the extent of this saving, and can employ the money in some much more profitable way. But if the whole class of farm-labourers could be persuaded to become teetotalers without substituting some new craving of equal force in the place of drink, it is extremely probable that in all places where there was an abundant supply of farm-labourers, the wage of a farm-labourer would gradually fall to the extent of the sum of money formerly spent in beer. For the lowest paid classes of labourers get, roughly speaking, no more wages than will just suffice to provide them with what they insist on regarding as necessaries of life. To an ordinary labourer "beer" is a part of the minimum subsistence for less than which he will not consent to work at all. Where there is an abundance of labour, as is generally the case in low-skilled employments, this minimum subsistence or lowest standard of comfort practically determines wages. If you were merely to take something away from this recognized minimum without putting something else to take its place, you would actually lower the rate of wages. If, by a crusade of temperance pure and simple, you made teetotalers of the mass of low-skilled workers, their wages would indisputably fall, although they might be more competent workers than before. If, on the other hand, following the true line of temperance reform, you expelled intemperance by substituting for drink some healthier, higher, and equally strong desire which cost as much or more to attain its satisfaction; if in giving up drink they insisted on providing against sickness and old age, or upon better houses and more recreation and enjoyment, then their wages would not fall, and might even rise in proportion as their new wants, as a class, were more expensive than the craving for drink which they had abandoned.

Or, again, take the case of technical or general education. In so far as technical education enabled a number of men who would otherwise have been unskilled labourers, to compete for skilled work, it will no doubt enable these men to raise themselves in the industrial sense; but the addition of their number to the ranks of skilled labour will imply an increase in supply of skilled labour, and a decrease in supply of unskilled labour; the price or wage for unskilled labour will rise, but the wage for skilled labour will fall assuming the relationship between the demand for skilled and unskilled labour to remain as before. A mere increase in the efficiency of labour, though it would increase the quantity of wealth produced, and render a rise of wages possible, would of itself have no economic force to bring about a rise. No improvement in the character of labour will be effectual in raising wages unless it causes a rise in the standard of comfort, which he demands as a condition of the use of his labour. If we merely increased the efficiency of labour without a corresponding stimulation of new wants, we should be simply increasing the mass of labour-power offered for sale, and the price of each portion would fall correspondingly. It would confer no more *direct* benefit upon the worker as such, than does the introduction of some new machine which has the same effect of adding to the average efficiency of the worker. Those who would advocate technical and general education, with a view to the material improvement of the masses, must see that this education be applied in such a way as to assist in implanting and strengthening new wholesome demands in those educated, so as to effectively raise this standard of living. There can be little doubt but that such education would create new desires, and so would indirectly secure the industrial elevation of the masses. But it ought to be clearly recognized that the industrial force which operates *directly* to raise the wages of the workers, is not technical skill, or increased efficiency of labour, but the elevated standard of comfort required by the working-classes. It is at the same time true, that if we could merely stimulate the workers to new wants requiring higher wages, they could not necessarily satisfy all these new wants. If it were possible to induce all labourers to demand such increase of wages as sufficed to enable them to lay by savings, it is difficult to say whether they could in all cases press this claim successfully. But if at the same time their efficiency as labourers likewise grew, it will be evident that they both can and would raise that standard of living.

In so far as the results of technical education upon the class of low-skilled labourers alone is concerned, it is evident that it would relieve the constant pressure of an excessive supply. Whatever the effect of this might be upon the industrial condition of the skilled industries subjected to the increased competition, there can be no doubt that the wages of low-skilled labour would rise. Since the condition of unskilled or low-skilled workers forms the chief ingredient in poverty, such a "levelling up" may be regarded as a valuable contribution towards a cure of the worst phase of the disease.

This brief investigation of the working of moral and educational cures for industrial diseases shows us that these remedies can only operate in improving the material condition of the poorest classes, in so far as they conduce to raise the standard of living among the poor. Since a higher standard of comfort means economically a restriction in the number of persons willing to undertake work for a lower rate of wage than will support this standard of comfort, it may be said that moral remedies can be only effectual in so far as they limit the supply of low-skilled, low-paid labour. Thus we are brought round again to the one central point in the problem of poverty, the existence of an excessive supply of cheap labour.

§ 5. **The False Dilemma which impedes Progress.**—There are those who seek to retard all social progress by a false and mischievous dilemma which takes the following shape. No radical improvement in industrial organization, no work of social reconstruction, can be of any real avail unless it is preceded by such moral and intellectual improvement in the condition of the mass of workers as shall render the new machinery effective; unless the change in human nature comes first, a change in external conditions will be useless. On the other hand, it is evident that no moral or intellectual education can be brought effectively to bear upon the mass of human beings, whose whole energies are necessarily absorbed by the effort to secure the means of bare physical support. Thus it is made to appear as if industrial and moral progress must each precede the other, a thing which is impossible. Those who urge that the two forms of improvement must proceed *pari passu,* do not precisely understand what they propose.

The falsehood of the above dilemma consists in the assumption that industrial reformers wish to proceed by a sudden leap from an old industrial order to a new one. Such sudden movements are not in accordance with the gradual growth which nature insists upon as the condition of wise change. But it is equally in accordance with nature that the material growth precedes the moral. Not that the work of moral reconstruction can lag far behind. Each step in this industrial advancement of the poor should, and must, if the gain is to be permanent, be followed closely and secured by a corresponding advance in moral and intellectual character and habits. But the moral and religious reformer should never forget that in order of time material reform comes first, and that unless proper precedence be yielded to it, the higher ends of humanity are unattainable.

CHAPTER X.

"SOCIALISTIC LEGISLATION."

§ 1. Legislation in restraint of "Free" Contract.—The direct pressure of certain tangible and painful forms of industrial grievance and of poverty has forced upon us a large mass of legislation which is sometimes called by the name of Socialistic Legislation. It is necessary to enter on a brief examination of the character of the various enactments included under this vague term, in order to ascertain the real nature of the remedy they seek to apply.

Perhaps the most typical form of this socialistic legislation is contained in the Factory Acts, embodying as they do a series of direct interferences in the interests of the labouring classes with freedom of contract between capital and labour.

The first of these Factory Acts, the Health and Morals Act, was passed in 1802, and was designed for the protection of children apprenticed in the rising manufacturing towns of the north, engaged in the cotton and woollen trades. Large numbers of children apprenticed by poor-law overseers in the southern counties were sent as "slaves" to the northern manufacturer, to be kept in overcrowded buildings adjoining the factory, and to be worked day and night, with an utter disregard to all considerations of physical or moral health. There is no page in the history of our nation so infamous as that which tells the details of the unbridled greed of these pioneers of modern commercialism, feeding on the misery and degradation of English children. This Act of 1802, enforcing some small sanitary reforms, prohibited night work, and limited the working-day of apprenticed children to twelve hours. In 1819, another Act was passed for the benefit of unapprenticed child workers in cotton mills, prohibiting the employment of children under nine years, and limiting the working-day to twelve hours for children between nine and sixteen. Sir John Cam Hobhouse in 1825 passed an Act further restricting the labour of children under sixteen years, requiring a register of children employed in mills, and shortening the work on Saturdays. Then came the agitation of Richard Oastler for a Ten Hours Bill. But Parliament was not ripe for this, and Hobhouse, attempting to redeem the hours in textile industries, was defeated by the northern manufacturers. Public feeling, however, formed chiefly by Tories like Oastler, Sadler, Ashley, and Fielden, drove the Whig leader, Lord Althorp, to pass the important Factory Act of 1833. This Act drew the distinction between children admitted to work below the age of thirteen, and "young persons" of ages from thirteen to eighteen; enforced in the case of the former attendance at school, and a maximum working week of forty-eight hours; in the case of the latter prohibited night work, and limited the hours of work to sixty-nine a week. The next step of importance was Peel's consolidating Factory Act of 1844, reducing the working-day for children to six and a half hours, and increasing the compulsory school attendance from two hours to three, and strengthening in various ways the machinery of inspection. In 1845 Lord Ashley passed a measure prohibiting the night work of women. In 1848, by the Act of Mr. Fielden, ten hours was assigned as a working-day for women and young persons, and further restrictions in favour of women and children were made in 1850 and 1853.

It must, however, be remembered that all the Factory legislation previous to 1860 was confined to textile factories— cotton, woollen, silk, or linen. In 1860, bleaching and dyeing works were brought within the Factory Acts, and several other detailed extensions were made between 1861 and 1864, in the direction of lace manufacture, pottery, chimney-sweeping, and other employments. But not until 1867 were manufactories in general brought under Factory legislation. This was achieved by the Factory Acts Extension Act, and the Workshops Regulation Act. For several years, however, the beneficial effects of this legislation was grievously impaired by the fact that local authorities were left to enforce it. Not until 1871, when the regulation and enforcement was restored to State inspectors, was the legislation really effectual. The Factory and Workshop Act of 1878, modified by a few more recent restrictions, is still in force. It makes an advance on the earlier legislation in the following directions. It prohibits the employment in any factory or workshop of children under the age of eleven, and requires a certificate of fitness for factory labour under the age of sixteen. It imposes the half-time system on all children, admitting, however, two methods, either of passing half the day in school, and half at work, or of giving alternate days to work and school. It recognizes a distinction between the severity of work in textile factories and in non-textile factories, assigning a working week of about fifty-six and a half hours to the former, and sixty hours to the latter. The exceptions of domestic workshops, and of many other forms of female and child employment, the permission of over-time within certain limitations, and the inadequate provision of inspection, considerably diminish the beneficial effects of these restrictive measures.

In 1842 Lord Ashley secured a Mining Act, which prohibited the underground employment of women, and of boys under ten years. In 1850 mine inspectors were provided, and a number of precautions enforced to secure the safety of miners. In 1864 several minor industries, dangerous in their nature, such as the manufacture of lucifer-matches, cartridges, etc., were brought under special regulations. To these restrictive pieces of legislation should be added the Employers' Liability Act, enforcing the liability of employers for injuries sustained by workers through no fault of their own, and the "Truck" legislation, compelling the payment of wages in cash, and at suitable places.

This slight sketch will suffice to mark the leading features of a large class of laws which must be regarded as a growth of State socialism.

The following points deserve special attention—

1. These measures are all forced on Parliament by the recognition of actual grievances, and all are testimony to the failure of a system of complete *laissez faire.*
2. They all imply a direct interference of the State with individual freedom—i.e. the worker cannot sell his labour as he likes; the capitalist cannot make what contracts he likes.
3. Though the protection of children and women is the strongest motive force in this legislative action, many of these measures interfere directly or indirectly with adult male labour—e.g. the limit on the factory hours of women and children practically limits the factory day for men, where the latter work with women or children. The clauses of recent Factory Acts requiring the "fencing of machinery" and other precautions, apply to men as well as to children and women. The Truck Act and Employers' Liability Act apply to male adult labour.

§ **2. Theory of this Legislation.**—Under such legislation as the foregoing it is evident that the theory that a worker should be free to sell his labour as he likes has given way before the following considerations—

(1) That this supposed "freedom to work as one likes" often means only a freedom to work as another person likes, whether that other person be a parent, as in the case of children, or an employer, as in the case of adult workers.

(2) That a worker in a modern industrial community is not a detached unit, whose contract to work only concerns himself and his employer. The fellow-workers in the same trade and society at large have a distinct and recognizable interest in the conditions of the work of one another. A, by keeping his shop

open on Sundays, or for long hours on week-days, is able to compel B, C, D, and all the rest of his trade competitors to do the same. A minority of workmen by accepting low wages, or working over-time, are often able to compel the majority to do the same. There is no labour-contract or other commercial act which merely regards the interest of the parties directly concerned. How far a society acting for the protection of itself, or of a number of its members, is justified in interfering between employer and workman, or between competing tradesmen, is a question of expediency. General considerations of the theoretic "freedom of contract," and the supposed "self-regarding" quality of the actions, are thus liable to be set aside by this socialistic legislation.

(3) These interferences with "free contract" of labour are not traceable to the policy of any one political party. The most valuable portions of the factory measures were passed by nominally Conservative governments, and though supported by a section of the Radical party, were strenuously opposed by the bulk of the Liberals, including another section of Radicals and political economists.

These measures signify a slow but steady growth of national sentiment in favour of securing for the poor a better life. The keynote of the whole movement is the protection of the weak. This appears especially in a recognition of the growing claims of children. Not only is this seen in the history of factory legislation, but in the long line of educational legislation, happily not ended yet. These taken together form a chain of measures for the protection of the young against the tyranny, greed, or carelessness of employers or parents. The strongest public sentiment is still working in this same direction. Recent agitation on the subject of prevention of cruelty to children, free dinners for school-children, adoption of children, child insurance, attest the growing strength of this feeling.

§ 3. **General extension of Paternal Government.**—The class of measures with which we have dealt recognizes that children, women, and in some cases men, are unable to look after their own interests as industrial workers, and require the aid of paternal legislation. But it must not be forgotten that the century has seen the growth of another long series of legislative Acts based also on the industrial weakness of the individual, and designed to protect society in general, adult or young, educated or uneducated, rich or poor. Among these come Adulteration Acts, Vaccination Acts, Contagious Diseases Acts, and the network of sanitary legislation, Acts for the regulation of weights and measures, and for the inspection of various commodities, licenses for doctors, chemists, hawkers, &c. Many of these are based on ancient historic precedents; we have grown so accustomed to them, and so thoroughly recognize the value of most of them, that it seems almost unnecessary to speak of them as socialistic measures. Yet such they are, and all of them are objected to upon this very ground by men of the political school of Mr. Herbert Spencer and Mr. Auberon Herbert. For it should be noted—

1. Each of these Acts interferes with the freedom of the individual. It compels him to do certain things—e.g. vaccinate his children, admit inspectors on his premises—and it forbids him to do certain other things.
2. Most of these Acts limit the utility to the individual of his capital, by forbidding him to employ it in certain ways, and hampering him with various restrictions and expenses. The State, or municipality, in certain cases—e.g. railways and cabs—even goes so far as to fix prices.

§ 4. State and Municipal Undertakings.—But the State does not confine itself to these restrictive or prohibitive measures, interfering with the free individual application of capital and labour, in the interests of other individuals, or of society at large.

The State and the municipality is constantly engaged in undertaking new branches of productive work, thus limiting the industrial area left open to the application of private capitalist enterprise.

In some cases these public works exist side by side in competition with private enterprise; as, for example, in the carriage of parcels, life insurance, banking, and the various minor branches of post-office work, in medical attendance, and the maintenance of national education, and of places of amusement and recreation. In other cases it claims an absolute monopoly, and shuts off entirely private enterprise, as in the conveyance of letters and telegrams, and the local industries connected with the production and distribution of gas and water. The extent and complexity of that portion of our State and municipal machinery which is engaged in productive work will be understood from the following description—

"Besides our international relations, and the army, navy, police, and the courts of justice, the community now carries on for itself, in some part or another of these islands, the post-office, telegraphs, carriage of small commodities, coinage, surveys the regulation of the currency and note issue, the provision of weights and measures, the making, sweeping, lighting, and repairing of streets, roads, and bridges, life insurance, the grant of annuities, shipbuilding, stockbroking, banking, farming, and money-lending. It provides for many of us from birth to burial—midwifery, nursery, education, board and lodging, vaccination, medical attendance, medicine, public worship, amusements, and interment. It furnishes and maintains its own museums, parks, art galleries, libraries, concert-halls, roads, bridges, markets, slaughterhouses, fire-engines, lighthouses, pilots, ferries, surf-boats, steam-tugs, life-boats, cemeteries, public baths, washhouses, pounds, harbours, piers, wharves, hospitals, dispensaries, gas-works, water-works, tramways, telegraph-cables, allotments, cow-meadows, artisans' dwellings, schools, churches, and reading-rooms. It carries on and publishes its own researches in geology, meteorology, statistics, zoology, geography, and even theology. In our colonies the English

Government further allows and encourages the communities to provide for themselves railways, canals, pawnbroking, theatres, forestry, cinchona farms, irrigation, leper villages, casinos, bathing establishments, and immigration, and to deal in ballast, guano, quinine, opium, salt, and what not. Every one of these functions, with those of the army, navy, police, and courts of justice, were at one time left to private enterprise, and were a source of legitimate individual investment of capital."[37]

Some of the utilities and conveniences thus supplied by public capital and public labour are old-established wants, but many are new wants, and the marked tendency of public bodies to undertake the provision of the new necessaries and conveniences which grow up with civilization is a phenomenon which deserves close attention.

§ 5. **Motives of "Socialistic Legislation."**—Stated in general terms, this socialistic tendency may be described as a movement for the control and administration by the public of all works engaged in satisfying common general needs of life, which are liable, if trusted to private enterprise, to become monopolies.

Articles which everybody needs, the consumption or use of which is fairly regular, and where there is danger of insufficient or injurious competition, if the provision be left to private firms, are constantly passing, and will pass more and more quickly, under public control. The work of protection against direct injuries to person and property has in all civilized countries been recognized as a dangerous monoply if left to private enterprise. Hence military, naval, police, and judicial work is first "socialized," and in modern life a large number of subsidiary works for the protection of the life and wealth of the community are added to these first public duties. Roads, bridges, and a large part of the machinery of communication or conveyance are soon found to be capable of abuse if left to private ownership; hence the post and telegraph is generally State-owned, and in most countries the railways. There is for the same reason a strong movement towards the municipal ownership of tramways, gas-and water-works, and all such works as are associated with monopoly of land, and are not open to adequate competition. In England everywhere these works are subject to public control, and the tendency is for this control, which implies part ownership, to develop into full ownership. Nearly half the gas-consumers in this country are already supplied by public works. One hundred and two municipalities own electric plant, forty-five own their tramway systems, one hundred and ninety-three their water supplies, at the close of 1902.

The receipts of local authorities from rates and other sources, including productive undertakings, had increased from seventy millions sterling to one hundred and forty-five millions between 1890-1 and 1901-2. Art galleries, free libraries, schools of technical education, are beginning to spring up on all sides. Municipal lodging-houses are in working at London, Glasgow, and several other large towns.

In every one of these cases, two forces are at work together, the pressure of an urgent public need, and the perception that private enterprise cannot be trusted to satisfy their need on account of the danger of monopoly. How far or how fast this State or municipal limitation of private enterprise and assumption of public enterprise will proceed, it is not possible to predict. Everything depends on the two following considerations—

First, the tendency of present private industries concerned with the supply of common wants of life to develop into dangerous monopolies by the decay of effective competition. If the forces at work in the United States for the establishment of syndicates, trusts, and other forms of monopoly, show themselves equally strong in England, the inevitable result will be an acceleration of State and municipal socialism.

Secondly, the capacity shown by our municipal and other public bodies for the effective management of such commercial enterprises as they are at present engaged in.

Reviewing then the mass of restrictive, regulative, and prohibitive legislation, largely the growth of the last half century, and the application of the State and municipal machinery to various kinds of commercial undertakings in the interest of the community, we find it implies a considerable and growing restriction of the sphere of private enterprise.

§ 6. The "Socialism" of Taxation—But there is another form of State interference which is more direct and significant than any of these. One of the largest State works is that of public education. Now the cost of this is in large measure defrayed by rate and tax, the bulk of which, in this case, is paid by those who do not get for themselves or for their children any direct return. The State-assisted education is said to tax A for the benefit of B. Nor is this a solitary instance; it belongs to the very essence of the modern socialistic movement. There is a strong movement, independent too of political partisanship, to cast, or to appear to cast, the burden of taxation more heavily upon the wealthier classes in order to relieve the poor. It is enough to allude to the income tax and the Poor Law. These are socialistic measures of the purest kind, and are directly open to that objection which is commonly raised against theoretic socialism, that it designs "to take from the rich in order to give to the poor." The growing public opinion in favour of graduated income tax, and the higher duty upon legacies and rich man's luxuries, are based on a direct approval of this simple policy of taking from the rich and giving to the poor.

The advocates of these measures urge this claim on grounds of public expediency, and those whose money is taken for the benefit of their poorer brethren, though they grumble, do not seriously impugn the right of the State to levy taxes in what way seems best. Whether we regard the whole movement from the taxation standpoint, or from the standpoint of benefits received, we shall perceive that it really means a direct and growing pressure brought to bear upon the rich for the benefit of the poor. A consideration of all the various classes of socialistic legislation and taxation to which we have referred, will show that we are constantly engaged more and more in the practical assertion and embodiment of the three following principles—

1. That the individual is often too weak or ignorant to protect himself in contract or bargain, and requires public protection.

2. That considerations of public interest are held to justify a growing interference with "rights of property."

3. That the State or municipality may enlarge their functions in any direction and to any extent, provided a clear public interest is subserved.

§ 7. Relation of Theoretic Socialism to Socialistic Legislation.—Now it has been convenient in speaking of this growth of State and municipal action to use the term Socialism. But we ought to be clear as to the application of this term. Although Sir William Harcourt declared, "We are all socialists to-day," the sober, practical man who is responsible for these "socialistic" measures, smiles at the saying, and regards it as a rhetorical exaggeration. He knows well enough that he and his fellow-workers are guided by no theory of the proper limits of government, and are animated by no desire to curtail the use of private property. The practical politician in this country is beckoned forward by no large, bright ideal; no abstract consideration of justice or social expediency supplies him with any motive force. The presence of close detailed circumstance, some local, concrete want to be supplied, some distinct tangible grievance to be redressed, some calculable immediate economy to be effected, such are the only conscious motives which push him forward along the path we have described. An alarming outbreak of disease registered in a high local death-rate presses the question of sanitary reform, and gives prominence to the housing of the working-classes. The bad quality of gas, and the knowledge that the local gas company, having reached the limit of their legal dividend, are squandering the surplus on high salaries and expensive offices, leads to the municipalization of the gas-works. The demand made upon the ratepayers of Bury to expend; £60,000 on sewage-works, a large proportion of which would go to increase the ground value of Lord Derby's property, leads them to realize the justice and expediency of a system of taxation of ground values which shall prevent the rich landlord from pocketing the contribution of the poor ratepayer. So too among those directly responsible for State legislation, it is the force of public opinion built out of small local concrete grievances acting in coalition with a growing sentiment in favour of securing better material conditions for the poor, that drafts these socialistic bills, and gets them registered as Acts of Parliament.

But the student of history must not be deceived into thinking that principles and abstract theories are not operative forces because they appear to be subordinated to the pressure of small local or temporal expediencies. Underneath these detailed actions, which seem in large measure the product of chance, or of the selfish or sentimental effort of some individual or party, the historian is able to trace the underworking of some large principle which furnishes the key to the real logic of events. The spirit of democracy has played a very small part in the conscious effort of the democratic workers. But the inductive study of modern history shows it as a force dominating the course of events, directing and "operating" the *minor* forces which worked unconsciously in the fulfilment of its purpose. So it is with this spirit of socialism. The professed socialist is a rare, perhaps an unnecessary, person, who wishes to instruct and generally succeeds in scaring humanity by bringing out into the light of conscious day the dim principle which is working at the back of the course of events. Since this conscious socialism is not an industrial force of any great influence in England, it is not here necessary to discuss the claim of the theoretic socialist to provide a solution for the problem of poverty. But it is of importance for us to recognize clearly the nature of the interpretation theoretic socialists place upon the order of events set forth in this chapter, for this interpretation throws considerable light on the industrial condition of labour.

We see that the land nationalizer claims to remove, and the

land reformer in general to abate, the evil of poverty by securing for those dependent on the fluctuating value and uncertain tenure of wage-labour an equal share in those land-values, the product of nature and social activity, which are at present monopolized by a few. Now the quality of monopoly which the land nationalizer finds in land, the professed socialist finds also in all forms of capital. The more discreet and thoughtful socialist in England at least does not deny that the special material forms of capital, and the services they render, may be in part due to the former activity of their present owners, or of those from whom their present owners have legitimately acquired them; but he affirms that a large part of the value of these forms of capital, and of the interest obtained for their use, is due to a monopoly of certain opportunities and powers which are social property just as much as land is. The following statement by one of the ablest exponents of this doctrine will explain what this claim signifies—

"We claim an equal right to this 'inheritance of mankind,' which by our institutions a minority is at present enabled to monopolize, and which it does monopolize and use in order to extort thereby an unearned increment; and this inheritance is true capital. We mean thereby the principle, potentiality, embodied in the axe, the spade, the plough, the steam-engine, tools of all kinds, books or pictures, bequeathed by thinkers, writers, inventors, discoverers, and other labourers of the past, a social growth to which all individual claims have lapsed by death, but from the advantages of which the masses are virtually shut out for lack of means. The very best definition of government, even that of to-day, is that it is the agency of society which procures title to this treasure, stores it up, guards and gives access to it to every one, and of which all must make the best use, first and foremost by education."

The conscious socialist is he who, recognizing in theory the nature of this social property inherent in all forms of capital, aims consciously at getting possession or control of it for society, in order to solve the problem of poverty by making the wage-earner not only a joint-owner of the social property in land but also in capital.

In other words, it signifies that the community refuses to sanction any absolute property on the part of any of its members, recognizing that a large portion of the value of each individual's work is due, not to his solitary efforts, but to the assistance lent by the community, which has educated and secured for the individual the skill which he puts in his work; has allowed him to make use of certain pieces of the material universe which belongs to society; has protected him in the performance of his work; and lastly, by providing him a market of exchange, has given a social value to his product which cannot be attributed to his individual efforts. In recognition of the co-operation of society in all production of wealth, the community claims the right to impose such conditions upon the individual as may secure for it a share in that social value it has by its presence and activity assisted to create. The claim of the theoretic socialist is that society by taxing or placing other conditions upon the individual as capitalist or workman is only interfering to secure her own. Since it is not possible to make any satisfactory estimate of the proportion of any value produced which is due to the individual efforts, and to society respectively, there can be no limit assigned to the right of society to increase its claim save the limit imposed by expediency. It will not be for the interest of society to make so large a claim by way of regulation, restriction, or taxation, as shall prevent the individual from applying his best efforts to the work of production, whether his function consists in the application of capital or of labour. The claims of many theoretic socialists transcend this statement, and claim for society a full control of all the instruments of production. But it is not necessary to discuss this wider claim, for the narrower one is held sufficient to justify and explain those slow legislative movements which come under the head of practical socialism, as illustrated in modern English history.

Now while this conscious socialism has no large hold in England, it is necessary to admit that the doctrine just quoted does furnish in some measure an explanation of the unconscious socialism traceable in much of the legislation of this century. When it is said that "we are all socialists to-day," what is meant is, that we are all engaged in the active promotion or approval of legislation which can only be explained as a gradual unconscious recognition of the existence of a social property in capital which it is held politic to secure for the public use.

The increasing restrictions on free use of capital, the monopoly of certain branches of industry by the State and the municipality, the growing tendency to take money from the rich by taxation, can be explained, reconciled, and justified on no other principle than the recognition that a certain share of the value of these forms of wealth is due to the community which has assisted and co-operated with the individual owner in its creation. Whether the socialistic legislation which, stronger than all traditions of party politics, is constantly imposing new limitations upon the private use of capital, is desirable or not, is not the question with which we are concerned. It is the fact that is important. Society is constantly engaged in endeavouring, feebly, slowly, and blindly, to relieve the stress of poverty, and the industrial weakness of low-skilled labour, by laying hands upon certain functions and certain portions of wealth formerly left to private individuals, and claiming them as social functions and social wealth to be administered for the social welfare. This is the past and present contribution of "socialistic legislation" towards a solution of the problem of poverty, and it seems not unlikely that the claims of society upon these forms of social property will be larger and more systematically enforced in the future.

CHAPTER XI.

THE INDUSTRIAL OUTLOOK
OF LOW-SKILLED LABOUR.

§ 1. **The Concentration of Capital.**—It must be remembered that we have been concerned with what is only a portion of the great industrial movement of to-day. Perhaps it may serve to make the industrial position of the poor low-skilled workers more distinct if we attempt to set this portion in its true relation to the larger Labour Problem, by giving a brief outline of the size and relation of the main industrial forces of the day.

If we look at the two great industrial factors, Capital and Labour, we see a corresponding change taking place in each. This change signifies a constant endeavour to escape the rigour of competition by a co-operation which grows ever closer towards fusion of interests previously separate.

Look first at Capital. We saw how the application of machinery and mechanical power to productive industries replaced the independent citizen, or small capitalist, who worked with a handful of assistants, by the mill and factory owner with his numerous "hands." The economic use of machinery led to production on a larger scale. But new, complex, and expensive machinery is continually being invented, which, for those who can afford to purchase and use it, represents a fresh economy in production, and enables them both to produce larger quantities of goods more rapidly, and to get rid of them by underselling those of their trade competitors who are working with old-fashioned and less effective machinery. As this process is continually going on, it signifies a constant advantage which the

181

owner of a large business capital has over the owner of a smaller capital. In earlier times, when trade was more localized, and the small manufacturer or merchant had his steady customers, and stood on a slowly and carefully acquired reputation, it was not so easy for a new competitor to take his trade by the offer of some small additional advantage. But the opening up of wider communication by cheap postage, the newspaper, the railway, the telegraph, the general and rapid knowledge of prices, the enormous growth of touting and advertising, have broken up the local and personal character of commerce, and tend to make the whole world one complete and even arena of competition. Thus the fortunate possessor of some commercial advantage, however trifling, which enables him to produce more cheaply or sell more effectively than his fellows, can rapidly acquire their trade, unless they are able to avail themselves of the new machinery, or special skill, or other economy which he possesses. This consideration enables the large capitalist in all businesses where large capital contains these advantages, or the owner of some large natural monopoly, who can most cheaply extract large quantities of raw material, to crush in free competition the smaller businesses. In proportion as business is becoming wider and more cosmopolitan, these natural advantages of large capital over small are able to assert themselves more and more effectively. In certain branches of trade, which have not yet been taken over by elaborate machinery, or where everything depends upon the personal activity and intelligence, and the detailed supervision of a fully interested owner, the small capitalist may still hold his own, as in certain branches of retail trade. But the general movement is in favour of large businesses. Everywhere the big business is swallowing up the smaller, and in its turn is liable to be swallowed by a bigger one. In manufacture, where the cosmopolitan character is strongest, and where machinery plays so large a part, the movement towards vast businesses is most marked; each year makes it more rapid, and more general. But in wholesale and retail distribution, though somewhat slower, the tendency is the same. Even in agriculture, where close personal care and the limitations of a local market temper the larger tendency, the recent annals of Western America and Australia supply startling evidence of the concentrative force of machinery. The meaning of this movement in capital must not be mistaken. It is not merely that among competing businesses, the larger showing themselves the stronger survive, and the smaller, out-competed disappear. This of course often happens. The big screw-manufacturer able to provide some new labour-saving machinery, to advertise more effectively, or even to sell at a loss for a period of time, can drown his weaker competitors and take their trade. The small tradesman can no longer hold his own in the fight with the universal provider, or the co-operative store.

But this destruction of the small business, though an essential factor in the movement, is not perhaps the most important aspect. The industrial superiority of the large business over the small makes for the concentration both of small capitals and of business ability. The monster millionaire, who owns the whole or the bulk of his great business, is after all a very rare specimen. The typical business form of to-day is the joint stock company. This simply means that a number of capitalists, who might otherwise have been competing with one another on a small scale of business, recognizing the advantage of size, agree to mass their capital into one large lump, and to entrust its manipulation to the best business ability they can muster among them, or procure from outside. This process in its simplest form is seen in the amalgamation of existing and competing businesses, notable examples of which have recently occurred in the London publishing trade. But the ordinary Company, whether it grows by the expansion of some large existent business, or, like most railways or other new enterprises, is formed out of money subscribed in order to form a business, represents the same concentrating tendency. These share-owners put their capital together into one concern, in order to reap some advantage which they think they would not reap if they placed the capital in small competing businesses. But though it has been calculated that about one-third of English commerce is now in the hands of joint stock companies, this by no means exhausts the significance of the centralizing force in capital. Almost all large businesses, and many small businesses, are recognized to be conducted largely with borrowed capitals. The owners of these debentures are in fact joint capitalists with the nominal owner of the business. They prefer to lend their capital, because they hope to enjoy a portion of the gain and security which belongs to a large business as compared with a small one. Along with this coming together of small capitals to make a large capital, there is a constant centralization and organization of business ability. It is not uncommon for the owner of a small and therefore failing business to accept a salaried post in the office of some great business firm. So too we find the son of a small tradesman, recognizing the hopelessness of maintaining his father's business, takes his place behind the counter of some monster house.

§ 2. How Competition affects Capital.—Now the force which brings about all these movements is the force of competition. Every increase of knowledge, every improvement of communication, every breakdown of international or local barriers, increases the advantage of the big business, and makes the struggle for existence among small businesses more keen and more hopeless. It is the desire to escape from the heavy and harassing strain of trade competition, which practically drives small businesses to suspend their mutual hostilities, and to combine. It is true that most of the large private businesses or joint stock companies are not formed by this direct process of pacification. But for all that, their *raison d'être* is found in the desire to escape the friction and waste of competition which would take place if each shareholder set up business separately on his own account. We shall not be surprised that the competition of small businesses has given way before co-operation, when we perceive the force and fierceness of the competition between the larger consolidated masses of capital. With the development of the arts of advertising, touting, adulteration, political jobbery, and speculation, acting over an ever-widening area of competition, the fight between the large joint stock businesses grows always more cruel and complex. Business failures tend to become more frequent and more disastrous. A recent French economist reckons that ten out of every hundred who enter business succeed, fifty vegetate, and forty go into bankruptcy. In America, where internal competition is still keener and speculation more rife, it has been lately calculated that ninety-five per cent, of those who enter business "fail of success." Just as in the growth of political society the private individual has given up the right of private war to the State, with the result that as States grow stronger and better organized, the war between them becomes fiercer and more destructive, so is it with the concentration of capital. The small capitalist, seeking to avoid the strain of personal competition, amalgamates with others, and the competition between these masses of capital waxes every day fiercer. We have no accurate data for measuring the diminution of the number of separate competitors which has attended the growing concentration of capital, but we know that the average magnitude of a successful business is continually increasing. The following figures illustrate the meaning of this movement from the American cotton trade, which is not one of the industries most susceptible to the concentrative pressure. "It will be seen that in 756 large establishments in 1880, in which the aggregate capital invested was five times as great as that in the 801 establishments in 1830, the capital invested per spindle was one-third less, the number of spindles operated by each labourer nearly three times as large, the product per spindle one-fourth greater, the product per dollar invested twice as large, the price of the cotton cloth nearly sixty per cent, less, the consumption *per capita* of the population over one hundred per cent greater, and the wages more than double. What is true of this industry is true of all industries where the concentration of capital has taken place."[38]

It is needless to add that these large works are conducted,

not by single owners, but in nearly all cases by the managers of associated capitals. Regarded from the large standpoint of industrial development, all these phenomena denote a change in the sphere of competition. From the competition of private capitals owned by individuals we have passed to the competition of associated capitals. The question now arises, "Will not the same forces, which, in order to avoid the waste and destruction of ever keener competition, compelled the private capitalists to suspension of hostility and to combination, act upon the larger masses of associated capital?" The answer is already working itself clearly out in industrial history. The concentrative adhesive forces are everywhere driving the competing masses of capital to seek safety, and escape waste and destruction, by welding themselves into still larger masses, renouncing the competition with one another in order to compete more successfully with other large bodies. Thus, wherever these forces are in free operation, the number of competing firms is continually growing less; the surviving competitors have crushed or absorbed their weaker rivals, and have grown big by feeding on their carcases.

But the struggle between these few big survivors becomes more fierce than ever. Fitted out with enormous capital, provided with the latest, most complex, and most expensive machinery, producing with a reckless disregard for one another or the wants of the consuming public, advertising on a prodigious scale in order to force new markets, or steal the markets of one another, they are constantly driven to lower their prices in order to effect sales; profits are driven to a minimum; all the business energy at their command is absorbed by the strain of the fight; any unforeseen fluctuations in the market brings on a crisis, ruins the weaker combatants, and causes heavy losses all round. In trades where the concentrative process has proceeded furthest this warfare is naturally fiercest. But as the number of competing units grows smaller, arbitration or union becomes more feasible. Close and successful united action among a large number of scattered competitors of different scales of importance, such as exist during the earlier stage of capitalism, would be impossible. But where the number is small, combination presents itself as possible, and in so much as the competition is fiercer, the direct motive to such combination is stronger. Hence we find that attempts are made to relieve the strain among the largest businesses. The fiercest combatants weary of incessant war and patch up treaties. The weapon of capitalist warfare is the power of under-selling—"cutting prices." The most powerful firms consent to sheathe this weapon, i.e. agree not to undersell one another, but to adopt a common scale of prices. This action, in direct restraint of competition, corresponds to the action of a trades union, and is attained by many trades whose capital is not large or business highly developed. Neither does it imply close union of friendly relations between the combining parties. It is a policy dictated by the barest instinct of self-preservation. We see it regularly applied in certain local trades, especially in the production and distribution of perishable commodities. Our bakers, butchers, dairy-men, are everywhere in a constant state of suspended hostility, each endeavouring indeed to get the largest trade for himself, but abiding generally by a common scale of prices. Wherever the local merchants are not easily able to be interfered with by outsiders, as in the coal-trade, they form a more or less closely compacted ring for the maintenance of common terms, raising and lowering prices by agreement. The possibility of successfully maintaining these compacts depends on the ability to resist outside pressure, the element of monopoly in the trade. When this power is strong, a local ring of competing tradesmen may succeed in maintaining enormous prices. To take a humble example—In many a remote Swiss village, rapidly grown into a fashionable resort, the local washerwomen are able to charge prices twice as high as those paid in London, probably four times as high as the normal price of the neighbourhood.

Grocers or clothiers are not able to combine with the same effect, for the consumer is far less dependent on local distribution for these wares. But wherever such retail combinations are possible they are found. Among large producers and large distributing agencies the same tendency prevails, especially in cases where the market is largely local. Free competition of prices among coal-owners or iron-masters gives way under the pressure of common interests, to a schedule of prices; competing railways come to terms. Even among large businesses which enjoy no local monopoly, there are constant endeavours to maintain a common scale of prices. This condition of loose, irregular, and partial co-operation among competing industrial units is the characteristic condition of trade in such a commercial country as England to-day. Competitors give up the combat *à outrance*, and fight with blunted lances.

§ 3. Syndicates and Trusts.—But it is of course extremely difficult to maintain these loose agreements among merchants and producers engaged in intricate and far-reaching trades. A big opportunity is constantly tempting one of them to undersell; new firms are constantly springing up with new machinery, willing to trade upon the artificially raised prices, by under-selling so as to secure a business; over-production and a glut of goods tempts weaker firms to "cut rates," and this breaks down the compact. A score of different causes interfere with these delicate combinations, and plunge the different firms into the full heat and waste of the conflict. The renewed "free competition" proves once more fatal to the smaller businesses; the waste inflicted on the "leviathans" who survive forms a fresh motive to a closer combination.

These new closer combinations are known by the names of Syndicate and Trust. This marks another stage in the evolution of capital. In the United States, where the growth is most clearly marked, the Standard Oil Trust forms the leading example of a successful Trust. In 1881, this Standard Oil Company having maintained for some ten years tolerably close informal relations with its leading competitors in the Eastern States, and having crushed out the smaller companies, entered into a close arrangement with the remaining competitors, with the view of a practical consolidation of the businesses into one, though the formal identity of the several firms was still maintained. The various companies which entered into this union, comprising nearly all the chief oil-mills, submitted their businesses to valuation, and placed themselves in the hands of a board of trustees, with an absolute power to regulate the quantity of production, and if necessary to close mills, to raise and lower prices, and to work the whole number as a joint concern. Each company gave up its shares to the Trust, receiving notes of acknowledgment for the worth of the shares, and the total profits were to be divided as dividend each half-year. This Trust has continued to exist, and has now a practical monopoly of the oil trade in America, controlling, it is reckoned, more than 90 per cent. of the whole market, and regulating production and prices.

Everywhere this process is at work. Competing firms are in every trade, where their small numbers permit, striving to come to closer terms than formerly, and either secretly or openly joining forces so as to get full control over the production or distribution of some product, in order to manipulate prices for their own profit. From railways and corn-stores down to slate-pencils, coffins, and sticking-plaster, everything is tending to fall under the power of a Trust. Many of these Trusts fail to secure the union of a sufficient proportion of the large competitors, or quarrels spring up among the combining firms, or some new firms enter into competition too strong to be fought or bought over. In these ways a large number of the Trusts have hitherto broken down, and will doubtless continue to break down. In England, this step in capitalist evolution is only beginning to be taken. In glass, paper, salt, coal, and a few other commodities, combinations more permanent than the mere Ring or Corner, and closer than the ordinary masters' unions, have been formed. But Free Trade, which leaves us open to the less calculable and controllable element of foreign competition, and the fact that the earlier stages of concentration of capital are not yet completed here in most trades, have hitherto retarded the growth of the successful Trust in England. Even in America there is no case where the monopoly of a Trust reigns absolute through the whole country, though many of them enjoy a local control of production and prices which is practically unrestricted. Excepting in the case of the Standard Oil Trust, and a few less important bodies which enjoy the control of some local monopoly, such as anthracite coal, the supremacy of the leading Trust or Syndicate is brought in certain places into direct conflict with other more or less independent competing bodies. In other words, the evolution of capital, which tends ever to the establishment of competition between a smaller number of larger masses, has nowhere worked out the logical conclusion which means the condensation of the few large competing bodies into a single mass. This final step, which presents a completely organized trade with the element of competition utterly eliminated under the control of a single body of mere joint-owners of the capital engaged, must be regarded as the goal, the ideal culmination of the concentrative movement of modern capital. It is said that more than one-third of the business in the United States is already controlled by Trusts. But most of them have only in part succeeded in their effort to escape from competition by integrating their personal interests into a single homogeneous mass. Even in cases where they do rule the market untrammelled by the direct interference of any competitors, they are still deterred from a free use of their control over prices by the possibility of competition which any full use of this control might give rise to. For it does not follow that even where a Trust holds an absolute monopoly of the market of a locality, that it will be able to maintain that monopoly were it to raise its prices beyond a certain point. In proportion, however, as experience yields a greater skill in the management of Trusts, and their growing strength enables them to more successfully defy outside attempts at competition, their power to raise prices and increase their rates of profit would rise accordingly.

Regarding, then, the development of the capitalist system from the first establishment of the capitalist-employer as a distinct industrial class, we trace the massing of capital in larger and larger competing forms, the number of which represents a pyramid growing narrower as it ascends towards an ideal apex, represented by the absolute unity or identity of interests of the capital in a given trade. In so far as the interests of different trades may clash, we might carry on this movement further, and trace the gradual agreement, integration, and fusion of the capitals represented in various trades. There is, in fact, an ever-growing understanding and union between the various forms of capital in a country. The recognition of this ultimate identity of interest must be regarded as a constant force making for the unification of the whole capital of a country, in the same way as the common interests of directly competing capitals in the same trade leads to a union for mutual support and ultimate identification.

§ 4. **Uses and Abuses of the Trust.**—This, however, carries us beyond the immediate industrial outlook. The successful formation of the Trust represents the highest reach of capitalistic evolution. Although the subject is too involved for any lengthy discussion here, a few points bearing on the nature of the Trust deserve attention.

The Trust is clearly seen to be a natural step in the evolution of capital. It belongs to the industrial progress of the day, and must not be condemned as if it were a retrograde or evil thing. It is distinctly an attempt to introduce order into chaos, to save the waste of war, to organize an industry. The Trust-makers often claim that their line of action is both necessary and socially beneficial, and urge the following points—

The low rates of profit, owing to the miscalculation of competitors who establish too many factories and glut the market; the waste of energy in the work of competition; the adulteration of goods induced by the desire to undersell; the enormous royalties which must be paid to a competitor who has secured some new invention—these and other causes necessitate some common action. By the united action of the Trust the following economic advantages are gained—

191

1. The saving of the labour and the waste of competition.
2. Economy in buying and selling, in discovering and establishing new markets.
3. The maintenance of a good quality of wares without fear of being undersold.
4. Mutual guarantee and insurance against losses.
5. The closing of works which are disadvantageously placed or are otherwise unnecessary to furnish the requisite supply at profitable prices.
6. The raising of prices to a level which will give a living basis of steady production and profit.

That all these economies are useful to the capitalists who form Trusts will be obvious. How far they are socially useful is a more difficult question. Reflection, however, will make one thing evident, viz. that though the public may share that part of the advantage derived from the more economical use of large capitals, it cannot share that portion which is derived from the absence of competition. If two or more Trusts or aggregations of capital are still in actual or even in potential competition, the public will be enabled to reap what gain belongs to larger efficient production, for it will be for the interest of each severally to sell at the lowest prices; but if a single Trust rule the market, though the economic advantage of the Trust will be greater in so far as it escapes the labour of all competition, there will be no force to secure for the public any share in this advantage. The advantageous position enjoyed by a Trust will certainly enable its owners at the same time to pay high profits, give high wages, and sell at low prices. But while the force of self-interest will secure the first result, there is nothing to guarantee the second and third. There is no adequate security that in the culminating product of capitalistic growth, the single dominant Trust or Syndicate self-interest will keep down prices, as is often urged by the advocates of Trust. It is true that "they have a direct interest in keeping prices at least sufficiently low not to invite the organization of counter-enterprises which may destroy their existing profits."[39] But this consideration is qualified in two ways:—*a*. Where Trust is formed or assisted by the possession of a natural monopoly, i.e. land, or some content of land, absolutely limited in quality, such potential competition does not exist, and nothing, save the possibility of substituting another commodity, places a limit on the rise of price which a Trust may impose on the public.. Although the fear of potential competition will prevent the maintenance of an indefinitely high price it will not necessarily prevent such a rise of price as will yield enormous profits, and form a grievous burden on consumers. For a strongly-constituted Trust will be able to crush any competing combination of ordinary size and strength by a temporary lowering of its prices below the margin of profitable production, the weapon which a strong rich company can always use successfully against a weaker new competitor.

But though a Trust with a really strong monopoly, and rid of all effective competition, will be able to impose exorbitant and oppressive prices on consumers, it must be observed that it is not necessarily to its interest to do so. Every rise of price implies a fall off in quantity sold; and it may therefore pay a Trust better to sell a large quantity at a moderate profit than a smaller quantity at an enormous profit. The exercise of the power possessed by the owners of a monopoly depends upon the proportionate effect a rise of price will have upon the sale. This again depends upon the nature and uses of the commodity in which the Trust deals. In proportion as an article belongs to the "necessaries" of life, a rise of price will have a small effect on the purchase of it, as compared with the effect of a similar rise of price on articles which belong to the "comforts" or "luxuries" of life, or which may be readily replaced by some cheaper substitute. Thus it will appear that the power of a Trust or monopoly of capital is liable to be detrimental to the public interest—1st. In proportion as there is a want of effective existing competition, and a difficulty of potential competition. 2nd. In proportion as the commodity dealt in by the Trust belongs to the necessaries of life.

§ 5. Steps in the Organization of labour.—The movements of labour show an order closely correspondent with those of capital. As the units of capital seek relief from the strain and waste of competition by uniting into masses, and as the fiercer competition of these masses force them into ever larger and closer aggregates, until they are enabled to obtain partial or total relief from the competitive strife, so is it with labour. The formation of individual units of labour-power into Trades Unions, the amalgamation of these Unions on a larger scale and in closer co-operation, are movements analogous to the concentration of small units of capital traced above. It is not necessary to follow in detail the concentrative process which is gradually welding labour into larger units of competition. The uneven pace at which this process works in different places and in various trades has prevented a clear recognition of the law of the movement. The following steps, not always taken however in precisely the same order, mark the progress—

1. Workers in the same trade in a town or locality form a "Union," or limited co-operative society, the economic essence of which consists in the fact that in regard to the price and other conditions of their labour they act as a complex unit. Where such unions are strongly formed, the employer or body of employers deals not with individual workmen, but with the Union of workmen, in matters which the Union considers to be of common interest.

2. Next comes the establishment of provincial or national relations between these local Unions. The Northumberland and Durham miners will connect their various branches, and will, if necessary, enter into relations with the Unions of other mining districts. The local Unions of engineers, of carpenters, &c., are related closely by means of elected representatives in national Unions. In the strongest Unions the central control is absolute in reference to the more important objects of union, the pressure

for higher wages, shorter hours, and other industrial advantages, or the resistance of attempts to impose reductions of wages, &c.

3. Along with the movement towards a national organization of the workers in a trade, or in some cases prior to it, is the growth of combined action between allied industries, that is to say, trades which are closely related in work and interests. In the building trades, for example, bricklayers, masons, carpenters, plasterers, plumbers, painters and decorators, find that their respective trade interests meet, and are interwoven at a score of different points. The sympathetic action thus set up is beginning to find its way to the establishment of closer co-operation between the Unions of these several trades. The different industries engaged in river-side work are rapidly forming into closer union. So also the various mining classes, the railway workers, civil servants, are moving gradually but surely towards a recognition of common interests, and of the advantage of close common action.

4. The fact of the innumerable delicate but important relations which subsist among classes of workers, whose work appears on the surface but distantly related, is leading to Trade Councils representative of all the Trade Unions in a district. In the midland counties and in London these general Trade Councils are engaged in the gigantic task of welding into some single unity the complex conflicting interests of large bodies of workmen.

5. An allusion to the attempts to establish international relations between the Unions of English workmen and those of foreign countries is important, more as indicating the probable line of future labour movement, than as indicating the early probability of effective international union of labour. Though slight spasmodic international co-operation of workers may even now be possible, especially among members of English-speaking races, the divergent immediate interests, the different stages of industrial development reached in the various industrial countries, seem likely for a long time at any rate to preclude the possibility of close co-operation between the united workers of different nations.

§ 6. Parallelism of the Movements in Capital and Labour.—
Now this movement in labour, irregular, partial, and incomplete
as it is, is strictly parallel with the movement of capital. In both,
the smaller units become merged and concentrated into larger
units, driven by self-interest to combine for more effective
competition in larger masses. The fact that in the case of capital
the concentration is more complete, does not really impair the
accuracy of the analogy. Small capitals, when they have co-
operated or formed a union, are absolutely merged, and cease
to exist or act as individual units at all. A "share" in a business
has no separate existence so long as it is kept in that business.
But the small units of labour cannot so absolutely merge their
individuality. The capital-unit being impersonal can be absolutely
merged for common action with like units. The labour-unit
being personal only surrenders part of his freedom of action
and competition to the Union, which henceforth represents the
social side of his industrial self. How far the necessity of close
social action between labour-units in the future may compel
the labourer to merge more of his industrial individuality in the
Union, is an open question which the future history of labour-
movements will decide.

The slow, intermittent, and fragmentary manner in which
labour-unions have been hitherto conducted even in the stronger
trades, is a fact which has perhaps done more to hide the true
parallelism in the evolution of capital and labour. The path
traced above has not yet been traversed by the bulk of English
working men, while, as has been shown, working women have
hardly begun to contemplate the first step. But the uneven rate
of development, in the case of capital and labour, should not
blind us to the law which is operating in both movements. The
representative relation between capital and labour is no longer
that between a single employer and a number of individual
working men, each of the latter making his own terms with the
former for the sale of his labour, but between a large company or
union of employers on the one hand, and a union of workmen on

the other. The last few years have consolidated and secured this relation in the case of such powerful staple industries in England as mining, ship-building, iron-work, and even in the weaker low-skilled industries the relation is gradually winning recognition.

§ 7. **Probabilities of Industrial Peace.**—This concentrative process at work in both capital and labour, consolidating the smaller industrial units into larger ones, and tending to a unification of the masses of capital and of labour engaged respectively in the several industries, is at the present time by far the most important factor of industrial history. How far these two movements in capital and in labour react on one another for peace or for strife is a delicate and difficult question. Consideration of the common interest of capital and labour dependent on their necessary co-operation in industry might lead us to suppose that along with the growing organization of the two forces there would come an increased recognition of this community of interest which would make constantly and rapidly for industrial peace. But we must not be misled by the stress which is rightly laid on the identity of interest between capital and labour. The identity which is based on the general consideration that capital and labour are both required in the conduct of a given business, is no effective guarantee against a genuine clash of interests between the actual forms of capital and the labourers engaged at a given time in that particular business. To a body of employés who are seeking to extract a rise of wages from their employers, or to resist a reduction of wages, it is no argument to point out that if they gain their point the fall of profit in their employers' business will have some effect in lowering the average interest on invested capital, and will thus prevent the accumulation of some capital which would have helped to find employment for some more working men. The immediate direct interests of a particular body of workmen and a particular company of employers may, and frequently will, impel them to a course directly opposed to the wider interests of their fellow-capitalists or fellow-workers. But it is evident that the smaller the industrial unit, the more frequent will these conflicts between the immediate special interest and the wider class interest be. Since this is so, it would follow that the establishment of larger industrial units, such as workmen's unions and employers' unions, based on a cancelling of minor conflicting interests, will diminish the aggregate quantity of friction between capital and labour. If there were a close union between all the river-side and carrying trades of the country, it is far less likely that a particular local body of dock-labourers would, in order to seize some temporary advantage for themselves, be allowed to take a course which might throw out of work, or otherwise injure, the other workers concerned in the industries allied to theirs. One of the important educative effects of labour organizations will be a growing recognition of the intricate *rapport* which subsists not only between the interests of different classes of workers, but between capital and labour in its more general aspect. This lesson again is driven home by the dramatic scale of the terrible though less frequent conflicts which still occur between capital and labour. Industrial war seems to follow the same law of change as military war. As the incessant bickering of private guerilla warfare has given way in modern times to occasional, large, organized, brief, and terribly destructive campaigns, so it is in trade. In both cases the aggregate of friction and waste is probably much less under the modern *régime*, but the dread of these dramatic lessons is growing ever greater, and the tendency to postponement and conciliation grows apace. But just as the fact of a growing identity in the interest of different nations, the growing recognition of that fact, and the growing horror of war, potent factors as they seem to reasonable men, make very slow progress towards the substitution of international arbitration for appeals to the sword, so in industry we cannot presume that the existence of reasonable grounds for conciliation will speedily rid us of the terror and waste of industrial conflicts. It is even possible that just as the speedy formation of a strong national unity, like that of Prussia under Frederick the Great, out of weak, disordered, smaller units, may engender for a time a bellicose spirit which works itself out in strife, so the rapid rise and union of weak and oppressed bodies of poorer labourers make for a shortsighted policy of blind aggression. Such considerations as this must, at any rate, temper the hopes of speedy industrial pacification we may form from dwelling on the more reasonable effects and teaching of organization. Although the very growth and existence of the larger industrial units implies, as we saw, a laying aside of smaller conflicts, we cannot assume that the forces at present working directly for the pacification of capital and labour, and for their ultimate fusion, are at all commensurate in importance with the concentrative forces operating in the two industrial elements respectively. It is indisputably true that the recent development of organization, especially of labour unions, acts as a direct restraint of industrial warfare, and a facilitation of peaceable settlements of trade disputes. Mr. Burnett, in his Report to the Board of Trade, on Strikes and Lock-outs in 1888, remarks *à propos* of the various modes of arbitration, that "these methods of arranging difficulties have only been made possible by organization of the forces on both sides, and have, as it were, been gradually evolved from the general progress of the combination movement."[40]

Speaking of Trade Unions, he sums up—"In fact the executive committees of all the chief Unions are to a very large extent hostile to strikes, and exercise a restraining influence"—a judgment the truth of which has been largely exemplified during the last two or three years. But our hopes and desires must not lead us to exaggerate the size of these peaceable factors. *Conseils de prud'hommes* on the continent, boards of arbitration and conciliation in this country, profit-sharing schemes in Europe and America, are laudable attempts to bridge over the antagonism which exists between separate concrete masses of capital and labour. The growth of piecework and of sliding scales has effected something. But the success of the Board of Conciliation and Arbitration in the manufactured iron trade of the north of

England has not yet led to much successful imitation in other industries. Recent experience of formal methods of conciliation and of sliding scales, especially in the mining, engineering, and metal industries, as well as the failure of some of the most important profit-sharing experiments, shows that we must be satisfied with slow progress in these direct endeavours after arbitration. The difficulty of finding an enduring scale of values which will retain the adherence of both interests amidst industrial movements which continually tend to upset the previously accepted "fair rates," is the deeper economic cause which breaks down many of these attempts. The direct fusion of the interests of employers and employed, and in some measure of capital and labour, which is the object of the co-operative movement, is a steadily growing force, whose successes may serve perhaps better than any other landmark as a measure of the improving *morale* of the several grades of workers who show themselves able to adopt its methods. But while co-operative distribution has thriven, the success of co-operative workshops and mills has hitherto been extremely slow. A considerable expansion of the productive work of the co-operative wholesale societies within the last few years offers indeed more encouragement. But at present only about 21/4 per cent. of English industry and commerce, as tested by profits, is under the conduct of co-operative societies. Hence, while it seems possible that the slow growth in productive co-operation, and the more rapid progress of distributive co-operation, may serve to point the true line of successful advance in the future, the present condition of the co-operative movement does not entitle it to rank as one of the most powerful and prominent industrial forces. Though it may be hoped and even predicted that each movement in the agglomerative development of capital and labour which presents the two agents in larger and more organized shape, will render the work of conciliation more peremptory and more feasible, it must be admitted that all these conciliatory movements making for the direct fusion of capital and labour, are of an importance subordinate to the larger evolutionary force on which we have laid stress.

We see then the multitudinous units of capital and labour crystallizing ever into larger and larger masses, moving towards an ideal goal which would present a single body of organized capital and a single body of organized labour. The process in each case is stimulated by the similar process in the other. Each step in the organization of labour forces a corresponding move towards organization of capital, and *vice versâ*. Striking examples of this imitative strategic movement have been presented by the rapid temporary organization of Australian capital, and by the effect of Dock Labourers' Unions in England in promoting the closer co-operation of the capital of shipowners. By this interaction of the two forces, the development in the organization of capital and labour presents itself as a *pari passu* progress; or perhaps more strictly it goes by the analogy of a game of draughts; the normal state is a series of alternate moves; but when one side has gained a victory, that is, taken a piece, it can make another move.

§ 8. Relation of Low-skilled Labour to the wider Movement.— The relation in which this large industrial evolution stands to our problem of the poor low-skilled worker is not obscure. In comparing the movement of capital with that of labour we saw that in one respect the former was clearer and more perfect. The weaker capitalist, he who fails to keep pace with industrial progress, and will not avail himself of the advantage which union gives to contending pieces of capital, is simply snuffed out; that is, he ceases to have an independent existence as a capitalist when he can no longer make profit. The laggard, ill-managed piece of capital is swept off the board. This is possible, for the capital is a property separable from its owner. The case of labour is different. The labour-power is not separable from the person of the labourer. So the labourer left behind in the evolution of labour organization does not at once perish, but continues to struggle on in a position which is ever becoming weaker. "Organize or starve," is the law of modern labour movements. The mass of low-skilled workers find themselves fighting the industrial battle for existence, each for himself, in the old-fashioned way, without any of the advantages which organization gives their more prosperous brothers. They represent the survival of an earlier industrial stage. If the crudest form of the struggle were permitted to rage with unabated force, large numbers of them would be swept out of life, thereby rendering successful organization and industrial advance more possible to the survivors. But modern notions of humanity insist upon the retention of these superfluous, low-skilled workers, while at the same time failing to recognize, and making no real attempt to provide against, the inevitable result of that retention. By allowing the continuance of the crude struggle for existence which is the form industrial competition takes when applied to the low-skilled workers, and at the same time forbidding the proved "unfittest" to be cleared out of the world, we seem to perpetuate and intensify the struggle. The elimination of the "unfit" is the necessary means of progress enforced by the law of competition. An insistence on the survival, and a permission of continued struggle to the unfit, cuts off the natural avenue of progress for their more fit competitors. So long as the crude industrial struggle is permitted on these unnatural terms, the effective organization and progress of the main body of low-skilled workers seems a logical impossibility. If the upper strata of low-class workers are enabled to organize, and, what is more difficult, to protect themselves against incursions of outsiders, the position of the lower strata will become even more hopeless and helpless. If one by one all the avenues of regular low-skilled labour are closed by securing a practical monopoly of this and that work for the members of a Union, the superfluous body of labourers will be driven more and more to depend on irregular jobs, and forced more and more into concentrated masses of city dwellers, will present an ever-growing difficulty and danger to national order and national health. Consideration of the general progress of the working-classes has no force to set aside this problem. It seems not unlikely that we are entering on a new phase of the poverty question. The upper strata of low-skilled labour are learning to organize. If they succeed in forming and maintaining strong Unions, that is to say, in lifting themselves from the chaotic struggle of an earlier industrial epoch, so as to get fairly on the road of modern industrial progress, the condition of those left behind will press the illogicality of our present national economy upon us with a dramatic force which will be more convincing than logic, for it will appeal to a growing national sentiment of pity and humanity which will take no denial, and will find itself driven for the first time to a serious recognition of poverty as a national, industrial disease, requiring a national, industrial remedy.

The great problem of poverty thus resides in the conditions of the low-skilled workman. To live industrially under the new order he must organize. He cannot organize because he is so poor, so ignorant, so weak. Because he is not organized he continues to be poor, ignorant, weak. Here is a great dilemma, of which whoever shall have found the key will have done much to solve the problem of poverty.

LIST OF AUTHORITIES.

By far the most valuable general work of reference upon *Problems of Poverty* is Charles Booth's *Labour and Life of the People* (Williams & Norgate). By the side of this work on London may be set Mr Rowntree's *Poverty: A Story of Town Life* (Macmillan). A large quantity of valuable material exists in *The Report of the Industrial Remuneration Conference*, and in the *Reports of the Lords' Committee on the Sweating System* and of the *Labour Commission.* Among shorter and more accessible works dealing with the industrial causes of poverty and the application of industrial remedies, Toynbee's *Industrial Revolution* (Rivington); Gibbins' *Industrial History of England (University Extension Series*, Methuen & Co.); and Jevons'*The State in Relation to Labour (English Citizen Series)*, will be found most useful. For a clear understanding of the relation of economic theory to the facts of labour and poverty, J.E. Symes' *Political Economy* (Rivington), and Marshall's *Economies of Industry*are specially recommended.

Among the large mass of books and pamphlets bearing on special subjects connected with *Problems of Poverty*, the following are most useful. An asterisk is placed against the names of those which deserve special attention, and which are easily accessible.

SWEATING AND ITS CAUSES.

* Booth, *Labour and Life of the People.*
* *Final Report of Lords' Committee on the Sweating System.*
Marx, "Capital," chap. xv., *Machinery and Modern Industry* (Sonnenschein).

Burnett, *Report to the Board of Trade on Sweating* (Blue-Book, 1887).

"Socialism," *Fabian Essays* (Walter Scott).

Booth, *Pauperism and the Endowment of Old Age* (Macmillan).

J. A. Spender, *The State and Pensions in Old Age* (Sonnenschein).

J. T. Arlidge, *Hygiene of Occupations* (Rivington).

CO-OPERATION AND LABOUR ORGANIZATION.

* Webb, *History of Trade Unionism* (Longman).
* Howell, *Conflicts of Capital and Labour* (Chatto & Windus).
* Burnett, *Report of Trade Unions* (Blue-Book).

Brentano, *Gilds and Trade Unions* (Trübner).

* Baernreither, *Associations of English Working-men.*

Acland and Jones, *Working-men Co-operators.*

Gilman, *Profit-sharing between Employer and Employed* (Macmillan).

Co-operative Wholesale Society's Annual.

Potter, *Co-operative Movement in Great Britain* (Sonnenschein).

* Webb, *Industrial Democracy* (Longman).
* Schloss, *Methods of Industrial Remuneration* (Williams & Norgate).

CHARTIABLE WORK AND POOR LAW, &C.

* Aschrott, *The English Poor Law System* (Knight).

H. Bosanquet, *The Strength of the People* (Macmillan).

P. Alden, *The Unemployed.*

Fowle, *The Poor Law* (*English Citizen Series*).
Booth, *In Darkest England.*
Blackley, *Thrift and Independence*
(People's Library, S.P.C.K.).
* Mackay, *The English Poor* (Murray).
* *Report on Pauperism in England and
Wales* (Blue-Book, 1889).
Rev. S.A. Barnett, *Practicable Socialism.*
Loch, *Charity Organization* (Sonnenschein).
*Report of Committee on National Provident
Insurance* (Blue-Book, 1887).

SOCIALISTIC LEGISLATION.

Ensor, *Modern Socialism* (Harpers).
* Jevons, *The State in Relation to Labour.*
Webb, *Socialism in England* (Swan Sonnenschein).
Hyndman, *Historical Basis of Socialism
in England* (Kegan Paul).
* "Socialism" (*Fabian Essays*).
* Toynbee, *Industrial Revolution* (Rivington).
Kirkup, *An Inquiry into Socialism* (Longman).

MOVEMENTS OF CAPITAL.

* Marx, "Capital," vol. ii., ch. xv.
* Baker, *Monopolies and the People* (Putnams).
"Socialism," *Fabian Essays.*
Macrosty, *Trust and the State* (Grant Richards).
Ely, *Monopolies and Trusts* (Macmillan).

The Measure of Poverty.

*Giffen, *Economic Inquiries and Studies* (Bell).

Mulhall, *Dictionary of Statistics* (Routledge).

Bowley, *National Progress in Wealth and Trade*(King).

* Board of Trade Memoranda, *British and Foreign Trade and Industrial Conditions* [cd. 1761 and 2237].

Statistical Abstract of the United Kingdom [cd. 1727].

* *Census of England and Wales: General Report*, 1901 [cd. 2174]. * Leone Levi, *Wages and Earnings of the Working-Classes* (Murray).

* *Report of the Industrial Remuneration Conference* (Cassell).

Giffen, *Growth of Capital* (Bell).

Valpy, *An Inquiry into the Conditions and Occupations of the People in Central London.*

FOOTNOTES

1. This sum includes an allowance for the part of the wage of domestic servants, shop-attendants, &c. paid in kind.
2. Leone Levi's *Wages and Earnings of the Working-Classes*, p. II.
3. *Labour and Life of the People*, vol. i. p. 38.
4. *Poverty: A Study of Town Life.* (Macmillan & Co.)
5. By Mr P.H. Mann in *Sociological Papers*. (Macmillan.)
6. Cf. *An Inquiry into the Conditions and Occupations of the People in Central London*, R. A. Valpy.
7. This statement is borne out by *A Return of Expenditure of Working-Men*, for 1889, published by the Labour Department of the Board of Trade.
8. See two interesting papers, "Our Farmers in Chains," by the Rev. Harry Jones (*National Review*, April and July, 1890).
9. Arnold White: *The Problems of a Great City*, p. 159.
10. Marshall's *Principles of Economics*, II. ch. iv. §2.
11. De Tocqueville, *Ancient Régime*, ch. xvi.
12. *Report of the Industrial Remuneration Conference*, 1886, p. 429.
13. Cannan's *Elementary Political Economy*, part ii. § 15.
14. *Industrial Remuneration Congress Report*, p. 153. Mr. W. Owen.
15. *Economics of Industry*, p. 111.
16. *Principles of Economics*, pp. 314, 316.
17. Kirkup, *Inquiry into Socialism*, p. 72.
18. Booth's *Labour and Life of the People,* vol. i. Part. III. ch. ii. *Influx of Population,* by H. Llewellyn Smith. A most valuable paper, from which many of the facts here stated have been drawn.
19. The official estimate is not precise, since our statistics of emigration refer only to non-European countries.
20. *Labour and Life of the People*, vol. i. p. 237.
21. *Labour and Life of East London*, vol. i. p. 224.
22. *Report on the Sweating System*, p. 14.
23. *Labour and Life of the People*, p. 271.

24. *Final Report on the Sweating System,* § 68.

25. *Lords' Committee on the Sweating System; Last Report,* p. 184.

26. *Labour and Life in London*, vol. i. p. 489.

27. Howell, *Conflicts of Capital and Labour,* p. 128. Second Edition, Macmillan & Co.

28. Karl Marx, *Capital*, vol. ii. p. 480.

29. *Labour and Life in East London,* vol. i. p. 112.

30. Cf. Howell's *Conflicts of Capital and Labour*, p. 207.

31. *The State in Relation to Labour*, p. 106.

32. *Problems of Greater Britain*, vol. ii. p. 314.

33. *Labour and Life of the People*, vol. i, p. 167.

34. The match-box trade, however, is chiefly in the hands of home-workers.

35. *Labour and Life of the People*, vol, i p. 427.

36. Roscher's *Political Economy*, § 242.

37. Fabian Essays in Socialism, p. 48.

38. Quoted by G. Gunton: *Political Science Quarterly*, Sept. 1880.

39. G. Gunton: *Political Science Quarterly,* Sept. 1888.

40. p. 17.

www.ingramcontent.com/pod-product-compliance
Lightning Source LLC
Chambersburg PA
CBHW030331270326
41926CB00010B/1580